YOUR SELF-SUFFICIENT BACKYARD HOMESTEAD GARDEN

A BEGINNER'S GUIDE TO GROWING FOOD AT HOME
AND CREATING A SUSTAINABLE POLLINATOR GARDEN
WITH ABUNDANT HARVESTS OF FRUITS AND
VEGETABLES

KAREN SHEPLEY

To my Mom in Heaven. You taught me to see beauty in life. With this book, I am sharing my passion for the beauty I see in mother nature.

To my Aunt, Sister, and Brother-in-Law, you are the wind beneath my wings. My appreciation and love for you will withstand the test of time and all the curveballs we dodge together.

To my family of friends who were on this book-writing journey with me, with all of my heart I appreciate each of you. I look forward to our friendships lasting a lifetime.

To my two puppies who are the most loving and amusing garden companions. Everything I do is for you. I love you to the moon and back a million times.

CONTENTS

Just For You

As a way of saying thank you for your purchase, I am offering you an additional very useful list of fruits, vegetables, companion plants, pollinator-loving plants, and pollinators to kickstart your own year-round garden that will bring you abundant harvests every month of the year.

Scan this code to receive instant access to *Companion Planting Chart for Fruits, Vegetables, and Pollinators.* I look forward to sharing your homestead and pollinator gardening journey with you.

HELPFUL WEBSITES

Dear Reader,

In this book, you'll find references to trusted gardening apps and sources for obtaining non-GMO and chemical-free seeds and plants.

To help you out on your gardening journey, I've compiled these sources here for easy access.

I hope you'll find them as helpful as I did.

Almanac Garden Planner

https://gardenplanner.almanac.com/

British Wildflower Seeds

https://britishwildflowermeadowseeds.co.uk/

Canadian Wildlife Federation

https://www.cwf-fcf.org/en/index.htm

Dobies

https://www.dobies.co.uk/

Greenhouse Garden Center

https://greenhousegardencenter.com/

Hardy Fruit Tree Nursery

https://www.hardyfruittrees.ca/

Landlife Wildflowers

https://www.wildflower.co.uk/

Native Food Nursery

https://nativefoodsnursery.com/

Natures Garden Seed Company

http://www.naturesgardenseed.com/index.php?location=Canada

Northern Wildflowers

https://northernwildflowers.ca/

Peaceful Valley Farm & Garden Supply

https://www.groworganic.com/

Prairie Moon Nursery

https://www.prairiemoon.com/

Prairie Nursery

https://www.prairienursery.com/

RHS

https://www.rhs.org.uk/

INTRODUCTION

The interesting smell coming from my friend's kitchen was enough to make my stomach churn. It only got worse when the fork filled with red cabbage came toward my mouth and the most annoying words to any fussy eater: "Just try it!" I knew I wasn't going to get out of it, so I closed my eyes and obeyed.

To my surprise, it was amazing. It tasted fresh and had just enough pepper to warm my taste buds but with a sweetness that made me ask for more. I couldn't work it out. I had been forced to eat all kinds of vegetables that I hated as a child, including red cabbage. My friend was beaming with pride as she told me that she had grown it in her garden, and the penny dropped. This was my first experience tasting home-grown, organic vegetables.

While I still can't stand people pressuring me to try different foods, thanks to my friend, I began an entirely new passion that day. What if all it took for me to eat more fruits and vegetables was for me to grow them myself? At the time, I only had a small balcony. But I wasn't going to let that put me off.

There is a devastating level of world hunger. As the population grows, the challenge to feed everyone becomes increasingly difficult. Farmers are turning to insecticides, rodenticides, and other harmful chemicals to provide bigger yields—but at the cost of human health.

Organophosphates are one of the most commonly used insecticides. These attack the enzymes that control nerve signals in insects. The Center for Disease Control warns us that these agents can have the same effects on people. What is sprayed onto crops doesn't just harm the insects. It seeps into the soil and can contaminate groundwater. Some chemicals are airborne and can spread much further than their targeted area.

The immediate concern might be the health consequences of eating crops that have been grown using these methods. The secondary, but no less significant, concern is what this is doing to our pollinators.

Pollinators such as bees, butterflies, birds, and other crucial insects are being killed off or left without habitat. In the attempt to create more food faster, we are destroying the homes of animals that play a vital role in our food production.

I say we as a society, not one person individually. Climate change is a complex topic that is not up for debate. I say we because each of us can make a small difference to help reverse some of the negative impacts mankind has had. And it all starts with our gardens.

> *"Even to the smallest creatures, we should have care and respect. They are here to help us not hurt us."*
>
> — APRIL PEERLESS

There is an incredibly good reason why Oprah Winfrey works on her own organic farm. It's not because she is rich, or because her wealth makes her an excellent gardener. Michelle Obama added a beehive to her organic garden and Morgan Freeman converted his 124-acre ranch into a bee sanctuary. All three could donate huge amounts of money to whatever cause they choose. However, they are setting tangible examples as they are aware of the important role pollinators have in the sustainability of our food supply. It's easy for the rich and famous to throw money at a problem. But they are setting positive examples to save pollinators, encouraging others to follow.

So many of you will be running through the list of reasons why homestead gardening isn't going to work for you.

Growing your own fruits and vegetables looks hard, maybe even expensive. There is the issue of time, and of course, space. Perhaps you have tried growing a few things and the only thing that sprouted was a weed. You may have even named yourself "black-thumbed" or the "killer of all things green."

I have certainly had my fair share of black-thumb disasters. Enthusiasm only took me so far. Still, this wasn't because I couldn't grow food for myself or for pollinators. I was just lacking the right knowledge. After ten years of trial and error and plenty of research, I'm so excited to be able to put all of this experience into a format that is both informative and effective.

We are going to discover exactly what pollinators are, why they are so crucial, and how we can use everyday materials to help them establish a home in your garden. To do this, we need to learn about native plants: those food supplies that will attract pollinators in your area. We will look into hardiness zones across the globe so that we can plant seeds that will flourish in particular climates. Whether you choose seeds or plants, you will find step-by-step guides to ensure they grow into strong, healthy plants that benefit the environment, as well as you.

When it comes to things like perennials, annuals, and companion plants, it's understandable that people get overwhelmed, especially when you read some information, get all motivated, and then realize the information has no relevance to your area. For the greatest successes in your homestead garden, planning is essential. Before even using the resources included to find reliable native seeds, we will work out the best design for the space you have so that you can incorporate a diverse range of fruits and vegetables.

With the help of seven steps to maintain your garden, with the least amount of work on your part, you are going to be amazed at just how much you can achieve—and without the use of any chemicals.

After reading this book, and with a splash of patience, you will be able to start small, watch the feedback, and understand any changes you need to make before adding to your plants and crops. I won't lie, homestead gardening isn't going to provide you with a juicy lemon next week. But, in the long run, you will develop a new love for nature, you will save money, and you will be healthier.

If that's not enough, the planet needs each one of us to start taking action. While the news of wildfires and floods makes its way into our homes, the extent of this damage is often overlooked. If you needed one more motivation to start growing your own food and creating a home for pollinators, this first chapter could be that final push.

WHY SHOULD WE BE GROWING OUR OWN FOOD AND CREATING HOMES FOR POLLINATORS

This chapter is not to make you feel guilty or as if you aren't doing your part. If you are reading this book, it's because you are passionate about becoming self-sufficient, providing healthy alternatives for your family and friends, and making a difference to the environment and the world. The problem is, while we know there is a need to grow our own food, not everyone realizes the importance of supporting pollinators, and not many people appreciate the severity. If you are like me, you probably have supermarkets lined with food, so it's hard to imagine not having a constant supply of food on the table.

HOW EXTENSIVE IS THE WORLD HUNGER PROBLEM?

According to the UN World Food Programme, there are 957 million people across ninety-three countries who don't have sufficient food. Furthermore, the Global Humanitarian Outlook estimates that there are 239 million people in need of life-saving action. In 2017, one in nine people on the planet was facing chronic food deprivation. To put that in perspective, consider how many people are in your extended family!

It is thought that climate change is one of the significant causes of the world hunger problem. Over the past few years, we have seen more and more natural disasters such as floods, wildfires, extreme heat, and droughts. These disasters are wiping out massive amounts of crops, affecting supply and demand. The irony is, we still call them natural disasters when pollution and contamination come from us humans. Burning fossil fuels and deforestation are said to be two of the biggest contributors to climate change, so are farming, and transportation. These pollutants change the Earth's atmosphere, causing temperatures to rise.

Sadly, politicians don't help. Globalization has allowed us to be able to buy practically anything from anywhere in the world. Yet, the political conflict between countries has a knock-on effect on global trade. Still, we won't just blame governments and inequality. Poverty also plays a role.

Not having enough food means people aren't getting the right nutrients. Without essential nutrients, minerals, and vitamins, health is worsened. People miss work and earn less money, so there is less income to buy food. It's a vicious cycle.

Here is what really hurts! Research shows that our food production is increasing faster than the global population, so much so that the world produces 1.5 times enough food for everyone around the globe (Food and Agriculture Organization of the United Nations, 2009).

So where is all this food going? Most of the industrially produced grain is used for biofuels and animal feed. Then, a third of the food produced is being lost or wasted. When you can pick up a bag of carrots for less than $1, it doesn't hurt if the odd one goes to waste. As soon as you start taking care to grow your own, it's amazing how nothing goes to waste.

QUANTITY AND QUALITY

The quantity of food isn't the only issue. Traditional farming methods that rely on chemicals can grow more food, but world hunger also includes the quality of the food. World hunger also includes providing the right nutrients. Approximately 45 percent of deaths that occur in children under five years old are connected to undernutrition (World Health Organization, 2021).

Because this is mainly in low- and middle-income countries, we aren't witnesses to it. Again, to put it into perspective, if you have children in school, what would 45 percent of their class look like?

It's not just the taste of organically grown food that is far superior. The nutritional levels are higher too. While organic tomatoes tend to be 40 percent smaller, they have more vitamin C, sugar, and lycopene. It's the sugar that adds to their flavor and, while we are aware of the benefits of vitamin C, lycopene can reduce the risk of stroke (PLOS ONE, 2013). The University of California found that organic tomatoes have nearly twice the amount of quercetin and kaempferol, flavonoids that are strong antioxidants.

Onions already have amazing health benefits. But organic onions have higher levels of gross phenol, gross flavonoid, vitamin C, and quercetin-3-glucoside. All of these are essential for a healthy gut.

Herbs and spices are especially easy to grow organically. They aren't just used to add flavor to dishes. Ginger is an excellent anti-inflammatory, as is garlic. Peppermint improves digestion and has antibacterial properties. Rosemary is full of antioxidants, it can boost circulation, and help improve memory. There are so many ways that we can boost our health from our own gardens.

Providing underdeveloped countries with the knowledge and resources to grow their own fruits, vegetables, herbs, and spices solve the problem of both quality and quantity.

ARE POLLINATORS REALLY ON THE DECLINE?

If you're walking through your garden or park and are attacked by flies or haunted by the buzzing of wasps, you might find it hard to believe that pollinators are on the decline. Again, part of this may be because of climate change, but it's the secondary effects that are causing the bigger problems.

Pollinators are losing their habitat because of natural disasters. There can be anywhere from 20,000 to 80,000 honeybees living in one hive. The ratio is two hives per acre. The US has suffered from horrendous wildfires, wiping out more than 7.8 million acres of land so far this year (National Interagency Fire Center, 2021).

On top of the loss of habitat, there are fewer areas for pollinators to forage and for nesting areas. Here is just why we should be concerned about the decline in pollinator numbers:

- From April 2020 to April 2021, US beekeepers lost 45.5 percent of their managed honeybee colonies (Auburn University, 2021).
- In Europe, around one-third of bee and butterfly

populations are on the decline and 10 percent of bee and butterfly species are endangered (European Parliament, 2021).

- Of the 11,000 bird species in the world, 4 out of 10 are on the decline (Bird Life International, 2018).

Sadly, because we only tend to see the damage insects do to crops, we feel the need to spray chemicals, nasty pesticides, and insecticides; to create barriers; and even to kill these animals that do far more good than harm. Caterpillars are the perfect example.

HANG ON A MINUTE—WE WANT CATERPILLARS?

Let's face it, the Hungry Caterpillar didn't just eat through one juicy leaf—he ate through every leaf. It's hard to see holey leaves in your garden as it can make you feel like the plant is unhealthy or diseased. The truth is, only a few caterpillar species are considered pests.

Remember: All caterpillars turn into butterflies or moths. Both of these are essential pollinators for your garden. Having a beautiful garden full of amazing butterflies outweighs the ugliness of a few holey leaves.

Caterpillars are also a food supply for wasps. Parasitic wasps lay their eggs on caterpillars and will feed off the caterpillar when they hatch. By exterminating caterpillars, you are removing a food source for wasps, another essential pollinator.

The next time you are tempted to use an insecticide, remember that this may likely wipe out beneficial caterpillars and not just the pests. Some people think it's a good idea to attempt to burn caterpillar tents. However, we really don't need the risk of more fires. The best solution is to dedicate an area of your garden to hungry caterpillars and other beneficial bugs. This way, they have a food supply and you have pollinators to make more food.

Try to remember that even caterpillars have the right to food. You can even spin it in a positive way and be proud that your leaves are so delicious!

WHY IS THIS EVERYONE'S PROBLEM?

So, going back to our lovely supermarkets that are stocked with a wide variety of foods; how is this everyone's problem? Depending on where you are in the world, you may have already started to see an increase in food prices. And even though it might be just a little bit here and a little bit there, your budget might be starting to tighten, or worse, it's becoming harder to make ends meet.

75 percent of global food crops rely on pollinators (United Nations, 2019). This includes fruits, vegetables, coffee, and cocoa, to name a few.

As pollinators decline, at least $235 billion of the world's annual crops could be at risk. This staggering amount of money will have to be recuperated in some manner. The likelihood of further increases in food prices is high. The cycle continues. Those who don't have access to sufficient nutritious food will suffer in terms of health. The current working generation might be ok but think about retirees, or students trying to live independently.

At some point, this is going to become a problem for everyone. Nevertheless, it's not all doom and gloom. There is a solution that everyone can be a part of.

HOW CAN YOU HELP?

Homestead gardening is the perfect way for each of us to make a difference. We can take advantage of the outdoor space we have and create a sanctuary for wildlife while providing a purpose—feeding the family. It's not the same as a farm garden that has crops in pretty rows but it can still be equally attractive, if not prettier!

A homestead garden takes advantage of space and natural elements to grow food and plants that will have multiple benefits. What you choose to grow will benefit you (and your pocket), they will benefit pollinators, and by choosing the right companions, they will benefit each other.

This is the main difference between gardening and homestead gardening. Gardening is the act of taking care of your garden. This can include mowing your lawn, pruning, watering, and taking control of those weeds. It doesn't necessarily mean "going green" and growing organic food. Gardening is a hobby. Homestead gardening is a hobby and a passion, even a lifestyle.

In the US, homestead gardening has been around since at least the 1700s. As there were no corner stores, people relied on what they could grow for both food and medicinal purposes. At the time, these were known as dooryard gardens.

Even during the early 1800s, the focus was on sustainability and not appearance. This meant that flowers came second after herbs, fruits, and vegetables. The dooryard gardens became known as kitchen gardens. When local produce markets began to open in the mid-1800s, home gardening became more of a hobby than a necessity.

In the late 1800s and early 1900s, three things caused homestead gardening to take a backseat. Grass became the fashion and so lawns were the latest thing. More people decided to live in urban areas because of the increase in manufacturing jobs. The role of the garden designer was created and there was more interest in native plants and flowers. This was further influenced by English garden designs that had a lot of perennials, larger lawns, and more shrub areas.

It was the food shortages during World War II that revived homestead gardening. Thanks to encouragement from President Roosevelt, there were 20 million homestead gardens by 1943, appropriately named "victory gardens."

Sadly, much of the interest was lost after the war. It wouldn't be until the early 2000s that the original dooryard gardens would become popular again. People started looking for healthier edibles that were both local and fresh. Once again, it was a president (or perhaps his wife!) who sparked a new interest when the first vegetable garden was planted in the White House in 2009.

Homestead gardening doesn't require the space or the money of a president. It will be daunting but there are several steps to homestead gardening that make life so much easier… and more productive.

If I could simplify these steps to the most basic, it would be the design, the integration, and the adaptation. That is to say, that before you rush to buy any seeds, you create a garden design that makes use of nature.

This is always going to be a small start. While homestead gardening isn't difficult, it is always best to start small and then integrate more once you know the best companion plants for your garden. The goal of integration isn't to fulfill our perfect design, but to take the design and add elements that copy nature.

You will have a list of things you want to grow in your garden, but not even gardens bow down to our wishes. By looking at what grows and what doesn't, we can adapt our design so that we are able to get the greatest yield.

With this in mind, we can expand the three basic principles into seven principles that are more specific:

1. Knowing what your homestead space has to offer in terms of water, light, and soil nutrients.
2. Starting small in order to plant more. This could be anything from replanting from containers to your garden to replanting your own seeds you have grown.
3. Taking care of your soil and finding natural ways to fertilize the soil.
4. Choosing the best companion plants to help with nutrients and natural pest control.
5. Selecting food you know you will use but also those that produce the highest yield.
6. Planning an irrigation system to feed your garden and pollinators but without creating too much work for you.
7. Maintaining your garden so that, each year, your homestead garden thrives because of what you have observed and learned.

We are going to take all of this to the next level to make sure we are supporting the crucial pollinators to find a home and help the planet.

Einstein was right about so many things. But he doesn't have to be right about the extinction of humans after four years without bees. With the right homestead garden design, we can all make our individual difference to a better world. And by growing our own food at the same time, there is so much satisfaction to be had.

Before you start to think about the fruits and vegetables you want to put on your table, let's take a look at the amazing range of pollinators that we can encourage into our outdoor spaces.

2

LEARN HOW TO IDENTIFY POLLINATORS

Before I began my homestead gardening experience, the word pollinators took me back to school and those biology lessons that explained how bees pollinate. Pollen from the male part of the flower sticks to the hair of the bee and is rubbed off onto the female parts of the next plant they visit.

If you have children, you might feel the urge to rush to their science books to brush up on this. Don't worry, we have included it all here!

For reproduction to take place, pollen needs to transfer from the male part of the plant, this is the long thin stems with little balls on top, called the stamen. Pollen passes to the stigma, the female part of the flower in the center. Some plants are self-pollinators. But, for an abundance of crops, we really need our pollinating insects and small mammal friends.

We all know that bees carry out this essential job, however, there are many other pollinators as well as some we can't even see. The wind can pollinate plants but, in sheltered gardens, the wind may not help. You can be a pollinator too. But the most effective are those that we will discuss in this chapter.

BIRDS

Bird pollination, officially known as Ornithophily, is necessary for more than sixty different flower families. One of the most amazing pollinators is the hummingbird, but as this little creature is only native to a certain area, we will come back to the "Pope of Pollinators", as I like to call them, soon.

New World orioles are actually related to the blackbird and not the Old World orioles. Adult males are a striking orange or yellow with a black head and wings. You will often see white on their wings. Females and young birds don't share the same vibrancy. There are 33 New World orioles genera (a rank that is above species but below family) that are generally found in the Americas, however, you might spot the odd one in Ireland and Great Britain. Eurasian Golden orioles are members of the Old World orioles and in summer, you can find these in Europe and parts of Western Asia.

As you can imagine from the name, Honeyeaters are awesome pollinators. Honeyeaters are native to Australia but can also be found in New Guinea, Tasmania, and New Zealand. There are a massive 190 species of Honeyeaters within 55 genera. With such a range of species, you can expect lots of different colors. Larger Honeyeaters can be black, gray, streaky brown, or dark green. The smaller species are more of an olive-green or brown and you might spot the odd yellow patch.

What I love about Honeyeaters is that they often hang upside down off a plant to feed on nectar. Some of the smaller species are able to hover like hummingbirds. To supplement their nectar diet, many honeyeaters also eat insects.

Sunbirds have a long beak, much like that of a hummingbird. As they tuck into the nectar of flowers, pollen gets stuck to their heads and necks. If they can't reach the nectar, they puncture a hole in the base of the flower. Of the 145 species, most are brightly colored, especially the males.

These small birds with short wings and long tail feathers can be found in Africa, Asia, and even across to the north of Australia. For those who aren't too keen on spiders, Sunbirds can help and many eat spiders; some even use their webs to help build nests.

When it comes to Europe and Antarctica, there are no specialized pollinating bird species. Studies have shown that there are 46 generalized bird species that visit flowers, such as the cyanistes, a member of the tit family. In the Mediterranean, pollination by birds is more common, especially as birds stop off during migration.

BEES

There are 300 species of mason bees in the Osmia genus. All of the Latin names of mason bees begin with "Osmia," which helps. The color range is impressive, some can be metallic blue or green, others are black, but my favorite is the Osmia bicolor for the amazing contrast of rusty red and black. Mason bees are found in the Americas, Asia, and Europe.

I love mason bees so much that they will be the next addition to my garden. People love keeping honeybees because of the honey they produce. Mason bees are far better pollinators, with one doing the work of sixty honeybees. If you have mason bees in your garden, 99 percent of the flowers will be visited compared to just 15 percent visited by honeybees. For homestead gardens, this means more fruits, vegetables, and flowers. On top of that, they are solitary bees, unlike the social honeybee.

Mason bees are also more "home creatures." From their nests, they will travel from 100 to 300 feet to choose their favorite flowers. Honeybees can travel for up to 2 miles. Beekeepers and homestead gardeners have more control over the area of pollination when keeping mason bees.

Their name comes from the fondness of using masonry products as homes, though they will also use mud. Some species will make homes in holes in wood and others are happy in the cracks of stones. Mason bees don't collect pollen with their back legs like other bees. They have special hairs across their abdomens that collect pollen.

Honeybees are popular because they produce both honey and beeswax. Strange yet fun fact, in some countries, the eggs and larvae are considered a delicacy and in other countries, adult honeybees are eaten. While fully respecting all cultures, I prefer to see my bees in the garden.

Honeybees are the most common type of bee and you can find them all over the world. Western honeybees are essential for food production but pollen is the only natural protein source for honeybees. Worker honeybees can consume between 3.4 to 4.3 milligrams of pollen each day.

Other important bees include squash bees. These are larger than honeybees and, if you are keen on growing cucumbers, squash, and watermelons, squash bees are crucial because all plants in the cucurbit group are pollinated by these bees. Squash bees collect pollen with their back legs.

Bumblebees can also be found all over the world and they are less aggressive than other types. The coolest thing about bumblebees is the way they pollinate. We associate the bumblebee with the loud buzzing sound they make. It's these fast vibrations that shake pollen over their entire body, so they are more efficient at pollinating than honeybees.

Leafcutter bees also deserve a mention. They are about the same size as a honeybee but they are darker in color. They have scissor-like jaws that cut through leaves and even flower petals. For this reason, like caterpillars, it's nice to have a special area for them in your garden. Male leafcutter bees don't have a stinger, nor are they great pollinators. The female rarely stings but she is an excellent pollinator thanks to the rows of pollen-collecting hairs on her abdomen. If a female leafcutter bee appears to have a yellow abdomen, you know she is covered in pollen.

BATS

The sun goes down and we head off to bed but the world of pollination stops for no one. As our daytime pollinators take some well-earned rest, it's time for bats to take over. And it's lucky they do. There are 528 plant species that rely on bats for pollination (Science Direct, 2019). At the same time, bats depend on the fruit and flowers of these plants for their own survival.

Fruit bats probably evolved in Australasia and can now be found in Europe, Asia, and Africa. Fruit bats, also known as megabats, are some of the largest bats, with some having a wingspan of up to 5.6 feet. That being said, many weigh around a third of the larger species. You can spot a fruit bat by their clawed second digit and their faces are similar to dogs and foxes.

The lesser long-nosed bats and the Mexican long-tongued bats have evolved into their role as pollinators. The tongue of the long-nosed bat is rough and ridged, making it ideal for taking in nectar, much like the Mexican long-tongued bat. The tongue of the lesser long-nosed bat is around 3-inches long and the Mexican long-tongued bat, around a third of its body length! Both these bats are able to hover like a hummingbird.

FLIES

I am the first person to admit that I look like a crazy person swinging my fly swatter around. I hate the thought of flies landing on my food. But, over the years, I have gained a new respect for them—in my garden.

We have all heard of busy bees, but flies are the second most important pollinators. This is because the 160,000 species all over the earth travel from plant to plant carrying the pollen with them. They just don't work so hard because adult flies don't require as much energy as bees. Flies can be specialized, seeking particular flowers, or generalized, choosing a variety of flowers. If you like chocolate, you might have to start liking these insects because they are critical for cocoa pollination.

The hoverfly looks very much like a wasp because of its color, however, it only has two wings compared with four. Hoverflies alone can pollinate more than 500 crop species. In Europe, they also significantly contribute to the pollination of wildflowers.

Fly species such as houseflies and blowflies have hair or bristles. As well as transporting pollen as they drink nectar, these types of flies will capture pollen on their bodies.

Biting midges also play an important role in pollination. Because of their minute size, they are one of the few insects that can access the depths of the flower and pollen that other insects can't reach.

BUTTERFLIES AND MOTHS

I feel that there is always a bit of discrimination when it comes to butterflies and moths. Butterflies are beautiful, colorful, dainty insects. Moths, on the other hand, are dull insects that just fly into your lights at night.

Butterflies aren't as effective at pollinating as bees. This is because their long legs keep their bodies away from the flower. Still, as adult butterflies only drink, they rely on nectar and are constantly "flower-hopping." Of the 17,500 butterfly species, the most important pollinator is the monarch butterfly. Fritillary and swallowtail butterflies should also be given some credit.

Now, moths can often be better pollinators. Some moths are nocturnal but others pollinate during the day. Many have the upper hand because they have hairy bodies and can transport more pollen. Furthermore, moths outnumber butterflies by more than ten to one. Hummingbird moths are the mini-me moth version of the hummingbird. The yucca plant wouldn't survive without the specially adapted mouth of the female yucca moth.

WASPS

It was a wasp expert that summed up this insect in a way that not only made sense but also made them a little more relatable. Wasps are incredibly intelligent. The problem is, their behavior is rather selfish and there is a touch of passive aggression. Nevertheless, wasps also have to visit many different flowers to support their high energy levels.

The yellowjacket wasp is probably the one that we are most familiar with. Yellowjackets and paper wasps are 2 of the 1,000 species that fall into the social wasp group. These wasps are stingers. They use their sting to hunt.

The other 29,000 species are solitary wasps and are non-stingers. That's not to say they don't have a sting, but they use it as a form of defense. Digger wasps and the great black wasp are pollinators that fall into this group.

BEETLES

Beetles can often be a little like butterflies and moths; a ladybug is cute, but we don't share the same admiration for your typical black scarab. Beetles may actually have been one of the world's first flower visitors, so for this, we should respect them and even thank them.

Because there are so many beetles, they make up the largest group of all pollinating animals. Of the 240,000 flowering plants in the world, beetles pollinate 88 percent.

Some beetles, like the ladybug, are able to fly. For this, they aren't considered pests because they can fly into the opening of the flower and collect pollen. Others are a little clumsy when it comes to the use of their wings and so they eat their way through the flower or they need a flower with a large opening.

Soldier beetles, soft-winged flower beetles, and scarabs are often considered the best pollinators. The ladybug is also a favorite, not just because it is cute but also because one ladybug can eat up to 5,000 aphids during its lifetime.

SMALL MAMMALS

Now that you have a better idea of how pollination works, it's easier to see how even small mammals can be pollinators. It only takes a mouse, rat, or shrew to pass a flower, capture pollen in their fur, and pass through other flowers for new plants, fruits, or veggies to grow.

Still, there are some small mammals that are classed as good pollinators. The largest pollinator in the world is actually the black-and-white ruffed lemur. They are able to use their hands to open flowers, their snouts and tongues to reach the pollen, and the pollen sticks to the fur on their faces.

From the largest pollinator to ants (which account for 10 percent of pollination), there is an amazing variety of pollinators in all corners of the planet. Some we fear, others we marvel, but all have their purpose and are essential. Before you start the next chapter, take a moment to grab a nice drink and sit in your garden. Even if it's just for a few minutes, see what pollinators are there. If you really struggle to find some, the next chapter will help you determine the changes you might make.

3

THE JOURNEY FROM EGG TO POLLINATOR

Anyone who has been pregnant and given birth, or been at a pregnant woman's side, will appreciate that it is one heck of a job! The last thing you need is someone annoying you or disturbing your home. Now imagine a female honeybee laying up to 2,000 eggs in just one day!

Understanding the life cycle of our pollinators helps us to identify where they might be nesting, how to take special care of these areas so as not to disturb them, and also how to make sure they have everything they need to mature and do their jobs.

We are going to take a look at the same groups of animals as in the previous chapter to understand their life cycles and to help choose plants that certain pollinators can't resist. That being said, we will skip the small mammals' group because I don't think we want to encourage rodents in our homestead gardens.

BIRDS

There are seven stages to the bird life cycle. We start with the egg. Some species lay only one egg but others more. The Gray Partridge can lay up to 20 eggs. The incubation period also differs depending on the size of the bird. For smaller birds, it takes an average of eleven to fourteen days and for larger birds, it could be a month. Once the chick uses its egg tooth to break out of the egg, it becomes a hatchling. The hatchling is ideal prey and it's a dangerous stage for them.

During the time that a hatchling spends developing, they are called nestlings. Most importantly at this stage, they are developing the ability to fly. Once their feathers and wings are fully developed, they take their first flight as fledglings. The juvenile and subadult stages are like the tweens and teens before becoming an adult bird ready to reproduce. Birds can live from one year to seventy years for larger birds and again, it very much depends on the species.

Birds love brightly colored flowers that are open during the day. The color is very important because birds have a terrible sense of smell. They like flowers that have tubes, funnels, and cups. They also need flowers that have strong supports to hold their weight, except those birds that can hover.

BEES

All bees go through four stages from egg to adult bee. The time it takes to become an adult and how long a bee lives will depend on its role. We will look at the honeybee for more detail. The queen honeybee lays an egg as small as a grain of rice in a hexagonal cell. Future queen bees have a special queen cell. If the egg is fertilized, it develops into a female worker bee and unfertilized eggs become male drones.

After three days, the eggs become larvae. Even larvae are fed different jellies depending on their role. Females get the worker jelly, drone jelly is for the male larvae, and only the finest royal jelly is for the future queen bee. As each larva grows, it spins a cocoon around itself while worker bees cover the cell with wax. This is the pupa stage and the larva develops into a bee. To enter the world, the bee chews its way out of the cell.

Another reason to love mason bees: the drone helps the worker bees to break out of the cell. Perhaps the bee equivalent of holding the door open.

From egg to adult worker bee takes between eighteen and twenty-two days whereas a drone takes twenty-four days. The queen bee leaves the cell after sixteen days. Generally speaking, drones live for an average of fifty-five days. Worker bees that are raised in the warmer months can live for six to seven weeks. If it's autumn, it can be as long as four to six months because there is less work to do. Healthy queen bees live for two years, or up to four years if she isn't replaced.

Bees like many of the same flowers as birds: those that are tubular and brightly colored. Bees can't see red, though. Instead, they have the amazing ability to see ultraviolet light. Flowers like the Mimulus have ultraviolet lines called nectar guides that help bees find their way to the nectar at the base of the tube. Bees like symmetrical flowers with large petals for landing. Unlike birds, bees like flowers that smell sweet or even minty. Interestingly, wild male bees favor different flowers from their female counterparts.

BATS

As the only flying mammal, the life cycle of a bat is very different from that of insects. The gestation period for bats is between fifty and sixty days. Female bats give birth to one baby, called a pup. For the first five weeks, these pups cling to their moms, even when they fly off to hunt.

After those first few weeks, the pups begin to learn how to fly. However, they will still return to the colony where mom roosted. It's not until they are about nine months to a year old that they become independent and mature.

Baby bats have a tendency to fly into homes and this isn't the nicest experience for you. But they will be genuinely terrified. If you are lucky to have bats in your area, consider having bat boxes in your garden so they can easily find their way back to their own home!

Bats live for an average of twenty years. There are six known species that have a lifespan of more than thirty years. The oldest recorded bat made it to forty-one years old!

Despite the phrase "blind as a bat," it's only the newborns that are blind. Just because they hunt with the use of vibrations, doesn't mean they can't see. In fact, some are able to see ultraviolet light like bees. It's not the color that attracts bats. They like very strong-smelling flowers and fruity smells. Because they are nocturnal, flowers need to be open at night and at least an inch in size, like Brugmansia or angel's trumpet.

FLIES

Flies also have a four-stage life cycle; the egg, larva, pupa, and adult. Flies only live for fifteen to thirty days. The problem is, they are considered pests because of the rate at which they reproduce. They like to lay eggs in warm, moist areas. An adult fly (twelve days old) can lay 100 eggs in one batch and more than 500 in a lifetime. Within 8 to 20 hours, the eggs hatch. Now in stage two, the larva is called a maggot. Maggots grow and shed their skin three times before they create a shell around themselves in the pupae stage. Inside the shell, they develop their wings, legs, and antennas.

Because flies love decaying food and waste, it's important to remember that if you want to make your own compost, you need to keep the heap away from doors and windows so you don't end up with flies inside.

Nature truly is amazing in its ability to adapt. Because flies like organic waste, they aren't drawn to the brightly colored, sweet-smelling flowers. They are attracted to things that literally look and smell like rubbish. For example, pawpaw has dark petals that are almost meat-colored. Red Trillium has bright red leaves, but it's the rotting-flesh smell that attracts flies.

This is actually a good thing. Imagine being at a buffet restaurant; you wouldn't want everyone going for the chicken wings. As flies like different flowers to birds and bees, it's easy to provide more diverse sources of food, making sure there is enough for everyone.

BUTTERFLIES AND MOTHS

The life cycle of the butterfly and the moth is the same. The female will lay eggs on a leaf. This is so that the larva that hatches has an instant food source. These caterpillars munch their way through leaves as they grow. Because the skin doesn't grow, caterpillars will shed their skin, or molt. The caterpillar attaches its tail to a stick or strong stem and starts preparing its home for metamorphosis. For butterflies, this is called a chrysalis and for moths, a cocoon. This pupa stage can take a few weeks before the adult emerges.

The time for each stage will depend on the species but more specifically, the weather. In spring, the life span from egg to adult can be ten to eleven months but in summer, it could be as short as one to four months. In extreme weather, it can be a lot longer. In the Arctic, some butterflies have a two-year life cycle. In the desert, larvae or pupae can hibernate for as long as seven years!

Butterflies are often drawn to flowers that produce a similar smell to what they produce to attract the opposite sex. They also like bright reds, yellows, and oranges. They like clusters of flowers that are open during the day as this gives them somewhere to land.

For monarch butterflies, milkweed is essential. Monarch caterpillars only feed on milkweed leaves. This is a very cool survival technique. The juice from these plants makes them taste horrible for predators.

Morning glories are ideal for both moths and butterflies because the nectar is hidden deeply. They open in the morning and don't close until the afternoon. Moths like plants that are open in the late afternoon and at night. Similar to butterflies, they like to land on clusters of flowers but they tend to be pale in color.

WASPS

After the queen wasp finishes hibernation in the spring, she starts building a few cells out of chewed wood and saliva. Here, she will lay eggs, feed the larvae, then seal the cell for the larvae to develop into pupae as the adult wasps leave the cell. Now that she has some worker wasps, they take over building new cells and the queen wasp lays around 200 to 300 eggs per day.

The colony grows incredibly quickly between then and the end of summer with anywhere between 5,000 and 10,000 wasps. At this point, the queen wasp produces new queens and fertile males. By autumn, the queen dies and the rest of the wasps leave the nest. Fertilized queen wasps find a place to hibernate for winter.

Blue, purple, yellow, and white flowers are preferred by wasps and they need to be open during the day and early evening. They also love fruit trees. But it's fig trees that need wasps and vice versa.

Fig wasps pollinate the 900 species of fig trees in a way that some people might find off-putting. If you are a fan of figs, you may want to skip down to beetles.

Inside a fig, there is an inflorescence, a small cluster of seeds and flowers. The female fig wasp makes her way inside the fig, lays her egg, and pollinates the flowers. Still inside the fig, the female dies and her egg hatches and develops into an adult fig wasp. Eating a wasp with every fig is not technically a myth, although enzymes in the fig will digest the female wasp.

BEETLES

Beetles also have four stages in their life cycle but interestingly, while beetles don't live for very long, the stages of the cycle are longer than that of bees and wasps. Female beetles lay hundreds of eggs at a time and it can take from four to nineteen days to hatch. As larvae, beetles can grow and shed their skin once or, for some species, this occurs up to thirty times.

During the pupae stage, beetles can remain in their cocoons for as long as nine months before leaving as fully developed adults. After this, beetles can live for as little as ten days to six months. The mayfly Dolania Americana is the beetle with the shortest lifespan of just five minutes. Ladybugs live for an impressive two years but the splendor beetle remains in the larva stage for over thirty years, so the longest living beetle award goes to this creature.

Beetles are a little less fussy when it comes to flowers. They are happy with single flowers and clusters and the flowers don't need to be high nectar producers. Beetles use their sense of smell to choose the best leaves to lay their eggs on, so the scent is important. They like spicy, sweet, and fermented-smelling flowers and they also have a fondness for bowl-shaped flowers like poppies and buttercups.

FOOD, SHELTER, AND WATER FOR ALL

Aside from nectar, many pollinators will also eat insects, which is ideal for creating a garden that both pollinates and controls its own pests. Birds control flies, beetles eat aphids, yellowjackets eat caterpillars, and so on.

By growing a garden that encourages a range of insects and pollinators, you are more likely to keep control over the potential damage that they can create. And to do this, you can make sure you are choosing a great range of plants and flowers.

But without shelter and water, your pollinators won't hang around for long. The shelter is relatively easy because insects will find shelter in long grasses, shrubs, and trees. Rock gardens are also excellent as they provide small cracks. I personally love the idea of spiral herb gardens using natural stones because you really get to make the most of space and extra shelter.

If you want to get really creative, you can make an insect home with materials you probably already have. If you have a couple of old pallets, you can cut them in half or quarters and stack them. If you have children or pets, you might want to nail the sections together so they don't fall. Then, in the spaces, use different items to loosely fill the gaps. Materials can include:

- Bamboo
- Sand
- Bricks
- Stones
- Pinecones
- Bark
- Leaves
- Twigs
- Small logs
- Straw

Remember to include a roof to protect the insect home from rain. You also need to find a location that provides shelter from the wind as well as some sun and shade.

As for water, a birdbath is a logical choice. However, as the name suggests this type of water supply is only really good for birds. Many insects won't be able to access the water and flying insects will find the surface area too slippery.

If you are going to include a birdbath, try to also include a secondary source of water. A simple bowl of water with some pebbles in it will be much appreciated by butterflies, bees, and wasps. At the end of my herb spiral, I used some smaller rocks to create a little rock pool so it blended in more as a natural look.

We have reached a point here where many people have a bit of a panic. You need twenty different flowers on top of your fruit and vegetables, then there is the task of building an insect house and what are you going to do if there is no space for shrubs? I know lots of people (and I have done this too) who rush out and start buying all sorts of plants because they need to save the bees!!

Enthusiasm is awesome but we can't let it get the better of us. More often than not, we plant too much at once and struggle to maintain it all correctly. This can really knock your confidence.

To set your homestead garden up for success, you need to introduce elements gradually. For this, the planning stage is one of the most crucial steps. While you may have an idea of what you want to grow, some plants will grow better in your climate than others. You are unlikely to get lovely ripe bananas growing in the English countryside! Your garden needs native plants and, to help you design the best homestead garden, we will look at these next.

4

YOUR GARDEN DESIGN AND THE IMPORTANCE OF NATIVE PLANTS

My first apartment had the tiniest little balcony with just enough space for two chairs. In one corner, I had a plant. Back in the day, I was a wannabe homestead gardener, and I bought the plant because it looked pretty, not because I knew what it needed or what it could provide in terms of food. In another corner, I grew mint. Now, this was my pride and joy because it was the first thing I had grown from seeds. It wasn't long before only one chair was needed, then no chairs because the plants were doing so well and overtook that little balcony.

From my balcony, I didn't have a wide variety of edibles. However, I did eventually have a pink flowering almond shrub, strawberries, cherry tomatoes, and an herb garden. My morning glory flowers were also my pride and joy as I used the balcony as a trellis and watched the pollinators pop in and out.

In this chapter, we are going to learn how to design your homestead space. The majority of this book is dedicated to gardens but here, we will also spend some time looking at how you can take advantage of any space. Regardless of the space you have, I can't stress how beneficial native plants are, so we will begin there.

WHY YOU NEED NATIVE PLANTS IN YOUR GARDEN

Native plants grow in an environment that is natural to them, without the need for us to intervene. Think about when you go for a walk in the countryside nearby, the amazing colors and smells around you are from the native plants. There are five main reasons why native plants will help your garden.

1. You will hardly have to water them

Because they have adapted to the climate, most native plants will survive on rainwater alone. If there is a particularly dry period, you might need to give them a little water, more so in their first year, but after that, they can cope with what nature provides. This is pretty magical for those who may forget to water the garden or even those who kill their plants with kindness and overwater them, like I used to do.

2. Native plants attract native wildlife

By introducing native plants, you are extending the natural habitat of native wildlife. A bird or a butterfly has little respect for a garden fence, so rather than not crossing into your garden, they will follow the trail of their preferred food, pollinating your garden. Native plants are also going to provide the ideal shelter for wildlife.

3. They don't need chemicals

Native plants grow well in their native climate. Aside from rainfall, all the nutrients they need can be found in the soil. This means there is no need for fertilizers or pesticides that might be needed for non-natives. It's not just about using chemicals in your garden. Rainwater runs off; the chemicals are taken with the rainwater and can end up in streams or rivers causing further damage to the wildlife and environment.

4. Native plants add to biodiversity

Every time land is developed, native plants are torn up and either replaced with buildings or people choose to landscape with non-native plants. This decreases the native species population and reduces diversity. Plant diversity is so important for keeping our air and water clean, to improve the quality of soil, and in return, provide us with better fruits and vegetables.

5. They are so much easier to maintain

By choosing native plants, you can save money on water and fertilizers and still enjoy a good harvest. Also, because they are designed to survive in the climate and with what nature provides them, there is less work for you.

WHAT CAN YOU DO IN THE SMALLEST OF SPACES?

If you don't have a huge garden you can still do your bit for pollinators and grow your own food. For those who have patios or balconies, there is still a good range of pollinators and edibles that will grow in containers.

If you are going to plant in containers, always use top-quality soil. This will help your plants get the right nutrients. You should remember that you will probably need to water the containers daily, possibly even twice during the hotter months. That being said, don't let them sit in a dish of water. Despite popular belief, plants won't just absorb the water throughout the day from the dish. It's more likely that you are then overwatering and you risk rotting the roots.

To make the most of each container, plant certain fruits, vegetables, or flowers together. You need to check that the plants have the same needs, including temperature, sunlight, and water. You wouldn't want to plant aloe vera (a desert plant) with the water-guzzling mint. The label of a plant or seed packet will have the necessary information. And we will look more at this when we talk about companion planting. You can find lots of inspiration for this by visiting the website, https://ebook.myhomesteadgarden.com, or scanning the code to the e-book Companion Planting Chart for Fruits, Vegetables, and Pollinators at the beginning and end of the book.

When choosing flowers, try to get the widest range of colors, shapes, and sizes so that your different pollinators are happy. Edibles that grow well in container pots include:

- Herbs like dill, mint, chives, rosemary, and bronze fennel
- Strawberries
- Raspberries
- Beans, using a trellis or balcony rails as a support
- Squash
- Patio-sized tomatoes
- Peppers/chilies

If you are completely new to homestead gardening, start small. Just choose a couple of things to grow so that you don't feel overwhelmed. You can always add to your garden once you are confident at reading plant signals and giving them what they need. Look ahead to the next season and plan to add a few more plants to boost your confidence and your harvest.

HOW TO START PLANNING YOUR GARDEN DESIGN

One of the most common mistakes people make is seeing space and filling it with what will look nice. Naturally, you want everyone to marvel at your garden but a correct design is a win-win situation. Your garden will look amazing and each element will be planted in the most beneficial area.

To begin, take a piece of paper and draw a rough outline of your garden including the house, paths, and any features that are permanent. We use zones to help design a garden, starting with Zone 0, which is your home. Zone 1 is closest to your home. Here, you will have your most frequently accessed edibles like an herb garden. After this comes Zone 2. Here, you can plant things that need regular attention, probably daily watering but you may not access them as often. Zone 3 is ideal for fruit trees and vegetables. You will probably need to visit this zone once or twice a week.

Zones 4 and 5 start to become a little wilder. The further away from your house, the less attention your plants will need. These areas are ideal for native plants, shrubs, insect hotels, etc. You can also choose these areas to grow some low-maintenance plants specifically for caterpillars and insects to lay their eggs. The less disturbance the better.

Two things to consider at this stage are the paths and the water supply. Edibles need to be planted where there is easy access to them. You don't want to have to trample over flower beds to pick your tomatoes every couple of days. If you aren't going to install any type of automatic irrigation system, the plants that need frequent watering should be in Zones 1 and 2 so that they are closer to a water supply.

There are no strict rules to these zones. For example, you might not go as far as Zone 5 which is complete wilderness. Your garden may end with a row of trees or shrubs, so more like a Zone 4. You may have a front and back garden, so the zones will extend around the entire house. A final consideration for each zone is the amount of sunlight each area gets— in summer and in winter. When you look at your seeds or young plants, you will need to match them with the right zone.

We still haven't looked at specifically what to plant in each zone. This is because the climate will have an impact and it's best to look at particular plants for your climate, which we will do soon.

WHAT ARE COMPANION PLANTS?

The best way to imagine companion plants is to think of a special person in your life who just fits! You might finish each other's sentences or you don't even need to talk because you know what each other is thinking. You are a better person with them around. Companion plants are two or more plants that support each other and grow better together.

I try to plan my companion plants based on three things. Of course, first of all, they will need to have the same growing requirements. Then, I look to see what nutrients a plant will need. The best companion plants will need different nutrients. Tomatoes and potatoes are from the same family. If you plant them together, they will absorb all the same nutrients and leave an excess of others. This will impact the quality of your soil and the tomatoes and potatoes.

Next, I look at plants that help each other out in terms of insect control. Certain plants will attract a particular pest. Planting two crops together that attract the same pest is like providing the pest with the main course and a dessert. So instead, you need to choose a companion plant that will help repel pests. The strong smell of mint next to your tomato plant will help keep pests away.

Sticking with tomatoes, there are also companion plants that can improve the flavor of your tomatoes. For example, thyme, chives, borage, basil, and even marigolds.

Traditional farming often has neat rows of crops. This is understandable for accessibility. However, in our gardens, we want to make sure as much of the available space is used. We can do that by planting different fruits, vegetables, herbs, and flowers together. In a perfect world, I would add a list of all the companion plants, but as you can imagine, that is an extensive list and will again depend on your climate. You can find lots of inspiration for this by visiting the website, https://ebook.myhomesteadgarden.com, or scanning the code to the e-book Companion Planting Chart for Fruits, Vegetables, and Pollinators at the beginning or the end of the book.

Let's take a closer look at some companion plants in general. Then, once you have looked at native plants for your climate, you can begin to finalize your garden design.

✿ Beans

Beans pair very well with peas, cabbage, beets, carrots, corn, and cucumbers. If you plant beans with nasturtiums or rosemary, you can keep away the bean beetles. Avoid garlic and onions next to beans.

✿ Carrots

You can plant carrots with your beans and rosemary because the rosemary will also deter carrot flies. Chives can also improve the flavor of carrots. Think about planting lettuce, onions, peas, peppers, and tomatoes with carrots but never dill.

✿ Potatoes

Despite their versatility, potatoes are a little bit fussy when it comes to making friends. Don't accompany your potatoes with asparagus, broccoli, cabbage, cauliflower, carrots, cucumbers, melons, peppers, raspberries, strawberries, or squash. You will be safe with basil, beans, celery, corn, garlic, onions, and marigolds. Horseradish can help prevent diseases too.

✿ Thyme

Thyme is like the best friend of the garden and pairs well with so many other plants that are beneficial to the garden. This includes other herbs like basil, chives, cilantro, and parsley but double-check the water requirements depending on the type of thyme because there are 300 types of thyme! You can also plant thyme with beans, blueberries, strawberries, cabbage-family crops, and shallots. If you have roses, plant thyme next to them to keep the aphids and black flies away.

✿ Lavender

Lavender is a wonderful plant for pollinators, especially bees, butterflies, and hover flies. Because of the strong smell, it also puts a lot of pests off. If you plant lavender with carrots or leeks, it will confuse unwanted insects. Purple Russian sage (or Lavender of Afghanistan) looks very much like lavender but it attracts bees like you wouldn't imagine, so it's a great alternative.

✿ Strawberries

Picking your own fresh strawberries is such a treat. You can help them out by planting them with bush beans, onions, lettuce, spinach, and squash. For herbs, think about chives or sage. Keep strawberries away from any of the cabbage family, eggplants, peppers, and tomatoes.

GIVING YOUR SEEDS THE BEST STARTING CHANCE

Seeds can be a little more challenging to grow because they can be sensitive to their environment. Tomato and marigold seeds are some of the easiest to plant so, for the absolute beginners, you may want to start here. So are basil and nasturtium seeds. Also, double-check the packet of each seed to make sure you plant the seeds at the right depth and that they have the right amount of sunlight and water.

1. Decide where you are going to plant your seeds

Some seeds, like the easy ones mentioned above, can be grown indoors and transplanted when the weather warms up. Poppies, beans, and squash are better planted outdoors. If your seed packet says "direct sow" they should be planted directly outdoors.

2. Choose ideal seed containers

Sometimes, it makes sense to buy seed containers because they have been designed to have the right drainage. Nevertheless, I am a big fan of recycling and using what you already have. Yogurt containers, egg cartons, and paper cups can have holes poked in the bottoms. Place them in any sort of tray such as a pie tin or casserole dish. I like using toilet paper roll holders because, once the seedling grows, you can plant the toilet paper roll straight into your soil and it will biodegrade. Cut slots in the base of the toilet roll and fold it in so that you make a base and the soil doesn't fall out.

3. Start with fresh soil

For the best chance of getting as many seedlings as possible, it's all about the soil quality. Your garden soil or reused container soil won't provide the same nutrients that seeds need. Start with fresh soil, tipped into a bucket. This will loosen up compact soil and aerate it. Add some water so that it is moist but not soaking wet.

4. Plant your seeds

Make two small holes in each container according to the required depth on the packet. Planting two seeds doubles your chances of success but no more because they need room and nutrients to grow. Cover the seeds with a little soil and use a mister to moisten the soil. You can use a watering can but one with fine holes so you don't accidentally drown the seeds.

5. Cover the seeds

This isn't always necessary but, if you want to help keep your seeds moist, a layer of plastic is like a comforting blanket on a cold day! At the first signs of germination, remove the plastic.

6. Feed your seedlings

The most important thing is going to be the right amount of water, again, preferably with a mister. A simple test to see if your soil is moist enough is to press the soil with a finger. If the soil sticks to your finger, it's moist. Some people like to add liquid fertilizer to help growth; I prefer adding some compost to the soil.

7. Give seedlings the right amount of light

Seedlings need between 14 and 16 hours of light a day. This means if you are growing them indoors, you might have to move them to a different window depending on the location of the sun. Try not to go over the 16 hours. More time doesn't mean healthier seedlings because they also need some dark in order to rest.

8. Slowly introduce indoor seedlings outside

Moving seedlings straight outdoors is going to be a shock to their little systems. A slow transition is called "hardening off" and gives them a chance to adapt and become stronger before transplanting. It normally takes seven to ten days to harden off seedlings and, whenever possible, take them outside when it's warmer.

9. Transplant your seedlings

If they are going into your soil, dig a hole slightly larger than the toilet paper roll. The hole should be deep enough to fit the entire roll. Add some compost to the base of the hole and slot the toilet roll in; fill any gaps with soil or a mixture of soil and compost. Don't forget to keep watering them. If you have been growing your seedlings in containers outdoors, the process is the same.

HOW TO REPLANT PLANTS FROM YOUR LOCAL NURSERY

If you aren't ready to start with seeds, and this is perfectly understandable, you might prefer to visit your local nursery and buy plants that are ready to replant into your garden. This could be flowers, vegetables, fruit trees, berries, or shrubs.

Early spring is the perfect time for this job. It may vary from plant to plant but the general rule of the green thumb is to wait until the last frost has passed. Many people will also replant in the mornings before direct sunlight hits the soil.

In many ways, the process is the same as for your containers. You need to dig a hole large enough to fit the container the plant is in. Again, make it a little larger so there is some wiggle room. You want to make sure that the hole is deep enough for the plant to sit at soil level.

Soil quality is again crucial at this stage. There must be adequate drainage and the soil needs to be of good quality. If necessary, add compost to the hole before you add the plant. Bear in mind that if you are going to add compost, you will need to dig a little deeper.

An excellent tip is to water the plant before taking it out of the container. This, and having the best soil, will reduce the chance of "transplant shock"—like the stress you experience when you move to a new house. Once you take the plant out of the container, check the roots. If they are all bundled up, you should gently loosen them before planting into the ground.

When the plant is in its new home, fill any gaps and very gently pat the soil. You might be tempted to give it a really good pat so that the plant is really well supported. Remember, if you pat too hard, you are compacting the soil and removing all the air, which the roots still need. Don't forget to water after replanting. This is especially important if you are replanting fruit trees. They need about an inch of water each week after replanting.

At this point, I also like to add a layer of mulch around the plant. Mulch can include leaves, bark, straw, or dry grass cuttings. The mulch will break down and feed the soil and also help retain moisture in the soil. Keep the mulch at least 1 foot away from the base of the plant or tree.

Now, my final piece of advice for this chapter is to control those emotions. I am always so desperate to get out there and stick my hands straight into the soil. Maybe you are excited, maybe nervous. Go back to your plan and keep updating it until you are happy. It's this planning stage and patience that will ensure the most amazing results. Even then, we still have the choice of perennials and annuals to maximize your homestead garden.

5

COMPLETING YOUR GARDEN FOR YEAR-ROUND RESULTS

S pring and summer are such amazing times of year. All of your efforts start to pay off and before you know it, your garden is full of life and color. You get to enjoy this energy, and of course the food for a few months, and then with the blink of an eye, fall becomes winter. The nights become longer, everything is colder, but worst of all, your garden seems to lose its vibrancy.

The next stage of our planning is to consider what we can plant to increase the chances of food for as many months of the year as possible. At the same time, we want to try and provide the perfect habitat for pollinators throughout the entire year. To do this, we increase the diversity by adding a mixture of perennials and annuals.

PERENNIALS AND ANNUALS—SELECTING A BIT OF BOTH

Another important piece of information on the back of your seed packet or on the plant label is whether your plant is a perennial or an annual. The name annual gives you quite a clue but these are the plants that have a short life cycle and will die off each season. Some will die because they reach maturity and others we harvest our crops from and the life cycle comes to a natural end. For this reason, annuals tend to be cheaper than perennials.

Perennials will survive through various harvests and even years. Some, especially fruit and nut trees, can live for decades. Olive trees are one of the hardiest perennials around with an average lifespan of 500 years. In fact, scientists have dated one olive tree in Spain to be 1,700 years old (CNN, 2017). This puts things in perspective. Creating a homestead garden can help you and future generations.

What's more, you will also save time and money in the long run but still get a good harvest. In their first year, they might need a little extra love and care but, if done right, they become quite hardy and require little maintenance. There is no need to buy seeds or seedlings each year, and then have to go through the initial planting process again.

If perennials are so great, why don't we just plant these? The majority of crops, especially the staples like rice and wheat, are annuals. Many homestead garden vegetables like corn, peas, and carrots are also annuals.

There are a few plants that like to confuse us. Take garlic as an example. It's a perennial that is most often grown as an annual. Garlic doesn't produce its own fertile seeds so new garlic can be grown from a clove. Typically, we harvest all of the garlic each year.

Because annuals and perennials each have their advantages, it makes sense to add both to your garden: perennials for easier gardening and annuals for a diverse harvest. And with the right planning to go with your design, you can plant fruit and vegetables to harvest in as many months of the year as possible.

We will look at an example of how you can plant crops for every season but don't feel the need to copy this idea because you still need to consider your climate.

- Spring: Asparagus, rhubarb, garlic, celery, kale, spinach, onions, carrots, potatoes, beets, lettuce
- Summer: Tomatoes, eggplants, cucumbers, squash, peppers, melons, raspberries, blueberries, strawberries, other members of the berry family
- Fall: Onions, leeks, fava beans, fruit and nut trees
- Winter: All herbs that can be started indoors

If you can plant one or two choices for each season, you are more likely to have a year-round food supply. Remember that spring and summer are the ideal times for planting but you should aim to plant something for every season. In fall, you may spend more time harvesting and in winter, the majority of plants go dormant.

Another way to make sure your table has homegrown food year-round is to look at different ways of preserving your food. Most vegetables can be frozen, except for potatoes and cabbage. Berries, apples, and lemons also do well frozen. When freezing fruit, make sure they are ripe or just ripe.

THE BEST ANNUAL PLANTS

The annuals that we are going to look at are relatively easy to grow in most climates. I love all of these because they are so versatile.

❁ Peppers

You can grow peppers and chilies in containers or in the ground. They like direct sunlight and well-drained soil. Peppers are strange ones because we treat them like annual vegetables because we sow, grow, and harvest, then the rest of the plant is turned into compost. But, as a close relative of the tomato, they are perennial fruits that will self-pollinate.

Choose a container that is at least 12 inches in diameter so the roots have room to grow. You might want to add some support because the peppers can weigh the branches down.

Your bell peppers should be ready within two to three months, chilies take a little longer.

✿ Onions

You don't even need seeds to grow onions unless you are looking for a specific type. If you cut the base of your onion and plant the base in the soil, new onions will grow from the cuttings. The cuttings will like plenty of water and should mature within 90 to 120 days.

If you're planting from seeds, plant them at about 6 inches under ground level and 12 inches apart. Again, the soil has to be kept moist because onions don't have long roots to absorb moisture from further down. Onions are good for those of us who lack patience because you can see the growth in just a few days.

✿ Kale

Kale is treated as an annual but it is a biennial, so it has a two-year life cycle. Kale is one of the hardiest vegetables for your garden. You can grow kale in containers, raised beds, or in the ground. As the goal is full leafy growth, they need more space, so plant seeds approximately 18 to 24 inches apart. Because kale grows quickly, you need to give it lots of water: 1 to 1.5 inches a week.

✿ Squash

Squash is fantastic for a big yield. Depending on the variety, you could be picking two or three squashes a day! Pay close attention to whether you have summer or winter squash. Summer squash is planted after the first frost whereas winter squash is planted in mid-summer. Their names come from the harvest time, not planting time.

Squash plants are sprawlers, so they need a good 3 to 6 feet. These vegetables need plenty of water; like kale, aim for 1 to 1.5 inches of water per week. Squash are normally full size when they get to 6 to 8 inches.

✿ Potatoes

I had better success with my potatoes when I used special potato bags, mainly because it makes them easier to harvest. If you are growing potatoes in a container, choose the smaller varieties.

Potatoes grow above the seed, so you need to plant the seed at least 6 inches into the ground and leave about 12 inches between each seed. As the plant grows above ground, you need to keep adding extra layers of soil so that only the top leaves are left uncovered. When the plants start to flower, you know your potatoes are ready for harvest.

✿ Carrots

Carrots love loose soil and they can handle frost, so it's often best just to plant them straight in the ground. While making sure the soil is loose, check that there is nothing in the soil (like stones) up to 12 inches deep that could block the growth of the carrots.

Plant seeds at about a quarter-inch deep and 2 to 3 inches apart in an area that receives plenty of sunlight. During spring, you can plant new carrot seeds every three weeks for a longer harvest. Be patient, it might be a few weeks before you see signs of growth.

THE BEST PERENNIAL PLANTS

For me, these are the plants that need the most consideration when it comes to choosing a location. This is because they are going to be around for some years and harvesting the fruits and vegetables needs to be convenient.

✿ Asparagus

Your asparagus can live for up to fifteen years. Seeds should be planted in spring 1 inch deep and 2 to 3 inches apart. It will be about three weeks before they germinate. Keep the soil moist and you can add a 6-inch layer of mulch over winter. It will take three years for asparagus to be ready for harvest. If you water well during the harvest period, you improve your chances of a bigger yield in drier years.

✿ Raspberries

There are 2 types of raspberries and if you plant both, you will have a longer harvest period. Summer-fruiting raspberries will give you one harvest in summer and ever-bearing raspberries can be harvested in fall and summer. It's more common that people buy plants rather than growing from seeds and provide some support, like a trellis.

Raspberries need lots of sunlight. The more sun they receive, the more fruit you get in return. In August, you also need to remember to prune the raspberry plant so that it keeps producing delicious berries.

✿ Strawberries

With strawberries, there are three harvesting varieties. June-bearing will give you strawberries for around three weeks. Ever-bearing can be harvested in summer and fall, however, the biggest yield is often in spring. Day-neutral strawberries aren't as fussy about getting as much sunlight and they will produce fruit until the first frost. Whichever type you decide on, pick strawberries first thing in the morning!

Plant strawberries 18 inches apart so that the runners have space. They will also need 1 to 1.5 inches of water per week and take care of your soil pH because strawberries like slightly acidic soil (5.5 to 6.8 pH).

✿ Dwarf trees

Dwarf trees can live for fifteen to twenty years. Despite the shorter lifespan, they are more convenient because they can be grown in the ground or a container. Just because they are small doesn't mean you can't get a good yield. Dwarf fruit trees can give you fifty lemons a year, around fifty to seventy apples, and forty to fifty nectarines.

Plant your dwarf trees where they can get 6 to 8 hours of sunlight a day. You only really need to water them once or twice a week, more in summer. What is most important is to prune the tree. It's best to do this in winter when it is dormant.

❀ Full-size trees

Fruit trees need the same care as dwarf trees. There are some advantages to full-sized trees. You get a greater yield and the fruit trees live longer, typically around thirty years. One of the biggest benefits is that these larger trees provide shade and shelter for our pollinator friends. Nevertheless, you need to have the space in your garden for a full-sized tree.

❀ Tomatoes

Generally speaking, plant tomato seeds about half an inch in the ground or container, and there should be around 15 inches of space between each plant. Because of the wide variety of tomatoes, double-check the packet for planting and watering. Tomato seeds will do well with a soil/compost mixture because they need a lot of nutrients. Plant seeds in late January and by May they should be ready to move into their permanent home. You will need to prune the tomato plant at the end of the season, but only the older leaves.

❀ Horseradish

Horseradish makes the list because it is still an easy plant to grow regardless of your climate. It likes the sun but will tolerate partial shade. Like carrots, you first need to prepare the soil so that nothing blocks the growth. You can grow horseradish from root cuttings. Plant the root between 2 and 3 inches below ground level, four to six weeks before the last frost. Horseradish has a tendency to spread, so you might want to plant it in containers.

THE BEST ANNUAL FLOWERS

We need to look at the 3 main types of annual flowers to help learn more about planting. If your soil is of good quality, you can plant hardy annuals straight into the ground or container, eight to ten weeks before the last frost. Half-hardy annuals can go into the ground after a hard frost. If you start them indoors, six to eight weeks before the last frost. Tender annuals can't be planted in the ground until all signs of frost have gone, or four to six weeks before the last frost if you are starting them indoors.

Here is a brief description of some fast-growing annual flowers for the enjoyment of both you and your pollinators.

✿ Marigold

The first signs of your bright yellow and orange blossom will only take about eight weeks after sowing the seeds. It's amazing that these flowers seem to thrive in poorer soil. Just be sure to have plenty of sunlight and good drainage.

✿ Morning glory

Morning glories are possibly my favorite trumpet flower. They can be white, purple, blue, and pink. They love the sun and the petals will open up once the morning sunlight reaches them.

✿ Sweet pea

I like sweet peas because they are happy climbing and make an ideal pair for beans. Sweet peas come in all sorts of colors from red to blue, lavender, and white. They also smell incredible. A good tip is to soak the seeds for a couple of days before you plant them.

✿ Nasturtium

This is actually a perennial but treated like an annual. The contrast of the orange petals and luscious green leaves is a favorite for butterflies and bees. What's more, it may take just a week for seedlings to appear, so another good choice if you struggle with patience.

✿ Sunflower

It's amazing how fast sunflowers grow. They can be as tall as you in just three months. They are surprisingly tough! Don't forget to harvest the seeds once the sunflower has died back, either to replant or as a nice snack.

✿ Cosmos

Cosmos flowers spread very easily and require little care. They are self-seeding so you can harvest the seeds to plant in spring. Although they are easy, they have a long, thin stem so are best in areas that are protected from the wind. Seedlings appear quickly but they won't blossom until later on.

✿ Bachelor's button

Bachelor's button is a self-seeding flower and is rather special for its true-blue color. It is very easy to grow, as long as seeds are planted in a sunny area and you should see the results fairly quickly. This is another favorite with pollinators, especially butterflies.

THE BEST PERENNIAL FLOWERS

Again, think about your long-term planning because these beauties should be around for a while. I like to take a bit of extra time thinking about which pollinators I can attract and the best companion plants too. Here are some excellent perennial flowers that can grow in most climates.

✿ Daisy

Did you know the name daisy comes from "day's eye" because the head of the flower closes at night and opens in the morning? The common daisy is yellow with white petals but there are another twenty-four different colors. Daisies are very easy to grow directly from the seed in your flowerbeds. All daisies need plenty of sunlight but check the packet for the best time of year to plant them depending on their variety.

❀ Foxglove

Some varieties of foxglove can grow up to 6 feet tall and, like many perennial flowers, they like well-drained soil in full sun or partial shade. The tubular clusters can be white, purple, pink, red, yellow, or lavender and they will blossom the second year after planting. If you don't cut the heads of foxgloves, they will reseed themselves.

❀ Comfrey

Comfrey is a good choice because it will grow in moist soil, sand, chalk, or clay, in full sun or partial shade. Bumblebees are a huge fan of comfrey. You can find purple, pink, and cream petals that flower between May and July.

❀ Garden angelica

Also known as wild celery, you can eat the stems and roots of garden angelica and it smells lovely. It's a tall plant with green flowers, so don't expect bright colors. However, it will attract solitary bees, wasps, and beetles, and the seeds are eaten by birds. Garden angelica likes moist soil in partial shade.

✿ Dandelion

Most people recognize this bright yellow flower because it grows so well in the wild across most of the northern hemisphere. Plant dandelions in the sun or partial shade and expect the flowers to bloom from April to June. Many types of bees like dandelions as well as beetles, and they serve as larval food for moths.

✿ Garden phlox

This is another very easy-to-grow perennial for beginners and has a lovely smell. For a real treat, choose the bicolor varieties but they also come with pink, white, purple, and orange petals. Sunlight is important but this particular flower also likes afternoon shade in warmer climates.

✿ Bee balm

As long as your soil is kept quite moist, bee balm is easy to grow. The flowers are vibrant reds, purples, and pinks and the plant can reach maturity in just three months. Bee balm will attract butterflies, hummingbirds, and bees and is considered a favorite of the honeybee. Remove the heads for better flowers next year.

WHAT IS CROP ROTATION?

The final part of our homestead garden planning and design is about crop rotation. Crop rotation enables you to choose specific plants that will benefit the soil depending on the needs of what was previously planted. Let's look at a simple example using a three-year crop rotation system.

- Year 1: In the first year, you have planted tomatoes, peppers, or potatoes. These plants are heavy feeders and will absorb a lot of the nitrogen in the soil. If you plant the same crop the following year, there might not be sufficient nitrogen for a healthy yield and you increase the chance of needing fertilizer.
- Year 2: After our heavy feeders, we want to restore the nitrogen in the soil. So, in the second year, you would plant a member of the legume family, say beans or peas. Legumes capture nitrogen in the atmosphere and convert it into beneficial nitrogen for other plants.
- Year 3: In the third year, you could plant a root crop such as carrots or parsnips. The long roots grow deeper to absorb nutrients further down and, at the same time, help to break up the soil ready to plant a heavy feeder the following year.

It sounds like an awful lot of planning, so once again, another reason to start simple. But because soil quality is so important, crop rotation is an excellent way of letting nature do what it does best.

You can see that gardening isn't difficult but it does require a lot of information and thought. If you are at this stage and your garden design isn't quite complete, or you are concerned that you are going to mess something up, there are some amazing apps that can help you—at least until you are in the swing of things.

Apps like Almanac Garden Planner take into consideration your climate to personalize your design. You can get all the information on growing guides and companion plants, and there are some useful videos too. You might just want to use a gardening app to check that your plan is going to be successful. Some people are still happy with a piece of paper and some colored markers plus a good calendar to help you remember. It's a personal choice.

Now that we have covered the general areas of homestead gardening, it's time to dig into the specifics of different climates. Let's start by looking at your best options for the US.

WILL YOU DO THE WAGGLE DANCE WITH ME?

"Hope is the only bee that makes honey without flowers."

— ROBERT GREEN INGERSOLL

I love the beauty and optimism in that sentence, but it's a tragic image when you take it literally. A bee *can't* make honey without flowers, and that little figurative bee of hope is almost too real of an image in the modern world.

Everyone deserves the flavor and nutrition of truly fresh produce, to know what it feels like to work with nature, to know how to look after themselves and the world around them. And I want to help make that happen.

So, I have a proposition for you: Let's be the bees.

Let's spread the pollen, the knowledge, and the skills. Help me to help other people access this lifestyle, and help pave the way for a brighter future.

No bee works alone. When one bee finds a good patch of pollen and nectar, she spreads the word to the colony, giving directions through a special dance known as the "waggle dance." The bee carries the scent of the flower patch she's visited, and she lets the other bees taste the nectar she's brought back.

She gives them a review, and because of that review, the whole colony benefits.

And that's what I'd like to ask you to do now (don't worry, you don't need to dance!).

All I'd like you to do is leave an honest review of your experience with this book.

Each review is a beacon for other people like you who want to do their best for themselves and for the environment.

Let's not hope without flowers. Let's fill the world with flowers, welcome the pollinators, and live as nature intended. And let's bring as many people along for the ride as possible.

Thank you for helping me with this. No bee works alone, and when we work together, we can truly become a colony.

Scan the QR code below to leave a review!

6

NATIVE PLANTS AND POLLINATORS IN THE US

S eeing how I have gone on about how native plants are so important, it only makes sense to look closer at particular regions around the world and narrow down the final selection of fruits, herbs, vegetables, and plants for your pollinators. Before we can even begin, you are going to have to find out which direction your garden will face.

For those in the northern hemisphere, the perfect garden will be facing south. This is because southern-facing gardens receive the most sunlight. As this isn't something you can exactly change, you may wonder if it is really significant. I would have to say yes because it can still help with your garden design. If you are choosing to plant crops together, you can take advantage of what is considered north and south so those plants that love the sun are getting more of it.

In the northern hemisphere, aim to plant from north to south. With your taller plants such as the beans on the most northern side, mid-range like your tomatoes in the middle, and onions to the south. This way, each element in your homestead garden gets the most amount of sunlight and a healthy amount of air circulation.

Needless to say, in the southern hemisphere, you have to plan for the opposite. Although the sun always rises in the east, in the northern hemisphere the north is to the left and in the southern hemisphere, the south is to the left. So, the golden ticket of homestead gardening down under is to have a north-facing garden.

Now let's get back to the US. I still laugh at myself and I welcome you to laugh too at this clumsy newbie gardener mistake. I was committed to creating the perfect design and I was working hard on my "zones." There were tons of pictures, notes, and sticky bits of paper attached to a corkboard in my kitchen. I started to see a bit of conflicting advice. Someone was suggesting I plant my chives in Zone 1, but the next article I read recommended Zone 5. And it wasn't only the chives where this trend was apparent.

The penny finally dropped and I learned that we have two different types of zones in the world of gardening. We have already looked at garden design zones that typically go up to 5 but can be higher. Now, we have to look at hardiness zones.

WHICH HARDINESS ZONE DO YOU LIVE IN?

In the US, there are thirteen hardiness zones, each broken down into a or b. Within each number, there can be a 10°F difference in temperature. It's not as simple as the north being colder than the south, although this is generally the case. You can imagine that mountains and deserts are going to change the average temperatures in some areas.

If you are living in Zone 4a, your minimum winter temperature would range from −30°F to −25°F. If you are in Zone 4b, it's a fraction warmer at −25°F to −20°F.

Zone	Temperature °F	Temperature °C
1	−60 to −50	−51 to −45.6
2	−50 to −40	−45.6 to 40
3	−40 to −30	−40 to −34.4
4	−30 to −20	−34.4 to −28.9
5	−20 to −10	−28.9 to −23.3
6	−10 to 0	−23.3 to 17.8
7	0 to 10	−17.8 to −12.2
8	10 to 20	−12.2 to −6.7
9	20 to 30	−6.7 to −1.1
10	30 to 40	−1.1 to 4.4
11	40 to 50	4.4 to 10
12	50 to 60	10 to 15.6
13	60 to 70	15.6 to 21.1

Understanding which one you are in can help you to choose the right plants that will survive the winter temperatures. It's also good for your confidence as this prevents you from planting things that aren't likely to grow.

That's not to say that plants with a hardiness Zone 5 won't grow in Zone 4. It just means that you are going to have to take more care of it. It might be safer to plant it in a container where it can be brought in for the winter or even just covered. At this stage, stick to your hardiness zone and, once you see some positive results, you can explore similar hardiness zones.

US NATIVE PLANTS

Your mind is probably going toward the "three sisters" we were all brought up on but there might be a couple of native US crops that surprise you.

✿ Corn

The first of the three sisters, corn is thought to be one of the oldest domesticated crops dating back around ten thousand years. The official name of corn is maize and it was the Mesoamericans that introduced the process of turning corn into flour. It is an annual plant.

Corn can be planted in hardiness Zones 4 through to 9 in areas with plenty of sunlight and it's best to plant directly outside. Apart from having nutrient-rich soil, corn needs the soil to be between 60°F and 65°F, so if you are in the colder zones, you may need to cover the soil with a layer of plastic to give the seeds a good chance. Plant the corn seeds 1 inch deep and 4 to 6 inches apart.

✿ Squash

Squash is great because of the winter and summer varieties of these three-sister crops. Summer squash varieties include straight neck, crooked neck, and zucchini. Butternut, spaghetti, and Hubbards are winter squash varieties. You can tell the difference because summer squashes are bushy and winter squashes are vine-growing.

Squash is an annual that can be planted in Zones 3 to 10. It's up to you whether you plant the seeds directly or start them off indoors if you want to get a few weeks ahead of the planting date. Plant seeds about 1 inch into the ground and, if you plant a few seeds together, don't forget to thin them out once they begin to grow. In warm weather, squash will grow quickly, so be sure to check them regularly. Summer squash should be harvested smaller when the skin turns glossy, but winter squash should be left to mature completely.

✿ Beans

Beans are the last of the three sisters and make a good companion plant for squash and corn. Corn stalks make good supports for bean vines. Again, because they are native, they grow well across most of the US in hardiness Zones 2 to 11.

It's most important with beans that you don't plant too early, so definitely wait for the spring. If the temperature is too cold or the soil is too moist, the seeds may rot. The ideal soil temperature is between 70°F and 80°F. Choose a spot in your garden that will give beans full sun. All beans should be planted at around 1 inch deep. Bushy bean seeds can be planted 1 to 2 inches apart but thinned out to 3 to 4 inches. For pole beans, plant a 6-

to 8-foot support first so you don't risk damaging the roots.

✿ Tomatoes

Long before the Italians were making pizza and pasta sauces, the indigenous people of South and Central America were growing tomatoes. The Amazon has 7,000 types of tomato plants that can be grouped into determinate and indeterminate. If you have limited space, stick to determinate because they tend to stop growing at about 3 to 4 feet.

You may struggle to grow tomatoes outdoors if you live in zones below 4 and over 11. More specifically, if you are in the north, tomato plants need a good 8 to 10 hours of sunlight but in the south, some shade in the afternoon will help. You can start seeds indoors or, if you are going for the direct approach, make sure the soil is at least 55°F, preferably 70°F. If you are transplanting, plant the tomato seedling in soil deeper than the container. You only need to leave the top leaves above ground level. Roots will grow from the stem and the plant will be stronger overall.

✿ Potatoes

Because of the famous Irish potato famine, many don't realize that it was actually the Incas that first cultivated potatoes, and 99 percent of cultivated potato varieties come from Chile. Folklore suggests you shouldn't plant your potato seeds until the first signs of dandelions, St. Patrick's Day, and even not until Good Friday so that the devil doesn't interfere. The truth is you can plant them as soon as the last chance of frost has passed.

Potatoes do well in Zones 1 to 7. In the north, check your soil temperature before planting. Once you are up to 50°F and the soil isn't too wet, you are good to go. In the warmer southern parts, you can even plant them as a winter crop. The easiest way to grow potatoes is to use a potato that has buds growing (those that you have left a little too long to eat). Once a potato has a few buds, they are known as seed potatoes. Cut them into golf ball size pieces with each one having at least two or three buds. Leave them for a couple of days.

Dig a small trench for your seed potatoes. How long you make it will depend on your garden but plan for one cut potato ball every 12 to 14 inches. The trench will need to be around 8 inches deep and 6 inches wide. Cover the seed potatoes with 3 to 4 inches of soil. When sprouts start to appear after about two weeks, add another 3 or 4 inches of soil and do the same again in a few weeks' time.

✿ Amaranth

Ten of the 75 amaranth varieties are native to North America. You can collect grain, which is often compared to quinoa, and the grain can be roasted like popcorn. You can also use the leaves of many species as a vegetable. Aside from being edible, amaranth has some lovely colored flowers from burgundy to orange and pinks.

In terms of zones, it will grow in Zones 2 to 11. It will grow in full sun or partial shade with moist soil but it should be well-drained. Amaranth is generally tall rather than bushy, so plant your seeds 10 to 18 inches apart. Because this plant has such amazing flowers, they look good close together as long as there is enough room for air circulation. They are self-seeding, so be prepared to thin the seedlings out in spring.

✿ Wild plums

American wild plums grow in practically all soil types but they prefer sand or clay. Many beginners will like this plant because it seems to do better when neglected. The fruit may be small but they are delicious and make great jams. You can grow American wild plums in partial shade from Zones 3 to 8. Small animals love to dig up seeds, so you are better building a barrier around the area where you will plant the seeds.

Loosen the soil around 12 inches deep and plant the plum seed at a depth of 4 inches. If you have harvested your own seeds, make sure they have been left to dry for at least a couple of weeks. Wild plums need a lot of water in the early days, approximately ten minutes in the morning and evening, bringing this down to just ten minutes in the morning. The tree will produce flowers from April to May and fruit from August to September.

✿ Red mulberries

Some will have a love-hate relationship with mulberries. They produce a lovely sweet fruit but if not harvested on time, they can be rather messy. Nevertheless, these berries also attract a lot of birds and honeybees. Red mulberries grow well in Zones 4 to 8.

Take a handful of red mulberries and soak them in water. The seeds that sink are the best seeds to plant. Remove these seeds, let them dry, and then place them in a bag with some sand. Leave them in your fridge for ninety days so they can chill. It is best to grow the seeds in a container for the first year. So, you just need to take one seed, brush off the sand, and plant it under a thin layer of soil. You don't need to place the container in direct sunlight but the daytime temperature needs to be around 80°F to 86°F. Once the plant is a year old, you can transplant it.

Mulberry trees are fast-growing but can take up to ten years to produce fruit. Some everbearing varieties produce fruit in just a year or two. Check state laws before getting excited about planting a mulberry tree. For example, El Paso, Texas and Phoenix, Arizona have banned planting new mulberry trees because they produce so much pollen!

✿ Crabapples

The difference between an apple tree and a crabapple tree is the size of the fruit. Apples that are smaller than 2 inches in diameter are crabapples. There are a number of varieties that will grow in Zones 3 to 9, so double-check you are choosing a variety for your zone.

Like mulberries, to plant crabapples from seeds, you need to go through the stratification process of chilling them for ninety days. After this time, cover the seeds with a thin layer of rich soil. Keep the seeds in full sunlight and you might even want to cover them with clear plastic to promote growth. Crabapples love the sun, so be sure to plant them somewhere that has sun all throughout the day. When the seedlings have grown to approximately 6 inches, you can plant them into separate containers and 12 inches means they are ready for their permanent home outdoors.

✿ Pawpaw

Pawpaw is a tropical fruit that is not to be confused with papaya. Pawpaw produces the largest fruit of all the native North American fruit trees. It can grow to approximately 6 feet and grown as either a tree or a dwarf tree. The fruit has a bit of a custardy taste.

This tree can be grown in Zones 5 to 9. They like a lot of sunlight but will need some shelter from the wind. Pawpaw doesn't self-pollinate. If you want fruit, you will need two cultivators (at least) planted at about 25 to 30 feet apart and helped out with some companion plants that will encourage pollinators. If you are transplanting, be sure to dig a hole at least 1 foot deep. One of the easiest ways to plant pawpaw is to take a ripe fruit and plant it whole in the ground, just under a thin layer of soil.

In spring, add a layer of mulch. The pawpaw tree will be low maintenance, only needing dead or broken branches to be pruned. From the seed, it will take about five to eight years for the tree to mature and three to eight years when transplanted. You should get a good harvest from mid-August to October.

WHAT NATIVE POLLINATORS CAN YOU EXPECT TO SEE IN YOUR GARDEN

It makes sense that the native pollinators are going to do a far better job pollinating plants, fruit, and vegetables than insects that have been introduced to the US. Native bees are one of the most important pollinators in the US especially for squash, tomatoes, cherries, blueberries, and cranberries. In fact, some native crops have a specialized species of bee to ensure their pollination.

There are 4,000 native bees in the US. Some are so small that you can barely see them, for example, the solitary Perdita minima at 0.07 inches. The largest native bees are often the carpenter bees at around 1 inch. Amazingly, it is estimated that 10 percent of native bees are still unnamed and undescribed.

Bats are also crucial for nighttime pollination. There are 45 bat species in the US, most of which prefer tropical areas.

Aside from pollinating, bats are very helpful for pest control, feasting on mosquitoes, fruit flies, and mayflies. If you are hoping for slightly smaller pollinators, you can hope to see parasitic wasps. Like bats, they help to maintain balance in a garden because they eat aphids and flies.

Sadly, many of the 750 butterfly species are at risk because of a loss of habitat. Native butterflies are grouped into six different families: skippers, blues and hairstreaks, brush-footed, swallowtails, whites and sulphurs, and metalmarks.

Of course, one of the most famous pollinators native to the American continents is the hummingbird. You can find them as far north as Alaska all the way down to Chile. The ruby-throated hummingbird is found in North America whereas many of the other species, like the sword-billed humming-bird are native to South America.

Bees may outnumber hummingbirds in the number of species but hummingbirds have a unique ability to pollinate that no other pollinator can. Many species of hummingbirds have a beak that ranges from 0.5 inches to 0.8 inches. The sword-billed hummingbird has a beak that can be 3.1 to 4.7 inches long. It's this beak that enables them to get to parts of a flower that no other insect can reach. The hummingbird's ability to pollinate is even more superior when you consider how the hummingbird hovers, flapping its wings at eighty beats per second, which helps to move the pollen. Having lots of red in your garden will help to attract hummingbirds.

THE BEST NATIVE FLOWERS TO ENCOURAGE POLLINATORS

At this point, I'm not going to create another section on how to plant each of these native flowers. I think you are well aware that the best thing to do is check your hardiness zone and the information on the back of the packet for the greatest success. Below, we have nine flowers that are native to the US and will encourage pollinators to your garden.

- **Purple coneflower:** This perennial has a large daisy-like head with long, thin petals. Overall, they can grow to a diameter of almost 5 inches. These flowers attract long-tongued bees and butterflies.
- **Lobelia:** Most of the lobelia plants are lovely blues and purples but you can find them in red too. Lobelia has been used as a medicinal plant to help with asthma and other breathing difficulties for centuries. Bees, butterflies, and hummingbirds love lobelia.
- **White sage:** It's a hardy plant but still needs plenty of care, especially water. Native Americans have used sage for healing and the ritual of burning sage is still popular in cultures today. White sage is another friendly choice for bees, butterflies, and hummingbirds.
- **Red twig dogwood:** I love this red, multi-stemmed bush with contrasting white flowers and berries. You

will also find this called red-osier dogwood. As well as birds, this perennial will attract small wildlife.

- **Elderberry:** American black elderberry is a shrub that can grow up to 13 feet and although the flowers are small, you can find clusters with hundreds of flowers. Not only is it a highly versatile edible, but American black elderberry is also popular with bees, wasps, beetles, birds, butterflies, and small mammals.

- **Trumpet vine:** Trumpet vines have lush green leaves that grow up to 4 inches long. In terms of our pollinator friends, the shape of these clusters along with the red-orange color is what makes them perfect for hummingbirds. Some care should be taken only because trumpet vines (or trumpet creepers) are invasive.

- **Milkweed:** As we have briefly seen, milkweed is essential for monarch butterflies for food as a host plant. There are 3 main types of milkweed— common, swamp, and butterfly—and all will grow across the US. There are lovely yellow, green, purple, pink, and orange flowers that attract monarchs and other butterflies as well as bees and hummingbirds.

- **Heliotrope:** Please be careful if you have cats or dogs as heliotrope is poisonous to them. Most of the flower clusters are purples and blues but you can find white heliotrope and red. Heliotrope is another good plant for monarch butterflies and hoverflies.

- **Delphinium:** This is possibly one of the most

amazing native plants for the US, at least for me.
Each spike can grow up to 6 feet with flowers
growing all around the spike right up to the top.
Bees, wasps, and hoverflies like the purple, blue, and
even white flowers.

This is just a taste of native plants in the US. There are more
than 18,000 to choose from so don't feel that you are limited
to these. While this list contains a good range of shapes and
colors, there will be other flowers that attract pollinators and
are suitable for your hardiness zone.

RESOURCES FOR NATIVE SEEDS AND PLANTS

I'm not saying that local nurseries aren't going to have good
quality seeds and plants but it is always great to have a few
contacts that offer native plants and that have an excellent
reputation.

My first stop for all my gardening needs is Greenhouse
Garden Center. They have stunning native plants and seeds,
but they also have some exceptional guides, and I am really
excited about the events they have coming up this year.

For edibles, I highly recommend Native Food Nursery. For
those who are conscious of plants that might be toxic to
insects, you can try Prairie Moon Nursery because all of
their plants are neonicotinoid-free. An online organic and
non-GMO source is Peaceful Valley. Peaceful Valley is a defi-

nite go-to source for me. This site has so much useful information and videos for learning about what you want to plant and how to care for them. Finally, Prairie Nursery has a massive range of seeds and plants in all categories for our pollinators. Their website is chock-full of information and I rate their customer service with five stars.

If you aren't sure where to buy your natives, these options are an excellent place to start. And without wanting to sound like a broken record, always check the plant information. You might think that accuracy isn't all that important but more so for first-time gardeners, confidence will grow as your plants do. Once your first set of plants starts to grow, you will learn so much from observation, making small changes to watering, soil conditions, and shade that you will be more prepared to plant things that might be considered more challenging.

7

HOW NATIVE PLANTS AND POLLINATORS VARY IN CANADA

E very country is beautiful in its own way but there is something about Canada that takes your breath away. The country is not generally associated with war, political scandals, or outrageous celebrities. Instead, you have stunning natural parks, wildlife, and of course, an amazing sense of peace. A homestead garden in Canada is a logical extension to the great outdoors many are privileged to experience.

CANADIAN ZONES 0 TO 9

I have heard various people say that the US and Canadian hardiness zones are the same or at least very similar. I think it's safe to say you will get a good idea but only compare the two as a rough guideline. The zones only go from 0 to 9 and they are separated into a and b. Being further north, you can imagine the temperatures are lower. Zone 0a starts at −70°F (−56.7°C) and the warmest average minimum temperature reaches 30°F (−1.1°C).

The US zones are based on minimum temperatures. The Canadian zones take into consideration the minimum temperatures, rainfall, the number of frost-free days, and a handful of other variables.

In Canada, there is also a much greater emphasis on microclimates. Let's say you have two gardens, both in Zone 4, but one has a 6-foot wall around it and the other doesn't. The garden with the wall will have more areas of shade but will also be protected from the wind. The same garden in Zone 4 without the wall will have a completely different microclimate. This makes sense considering Canada has the longest coastline in the world at 125,556 miles (202,063 kilometers). The extensive coastline and having more lakes than any other country in the world means there is a lot more to consider than just minimum temperatures.

To give you an idea of how the Canadian hardiness zones differ from the US zones, a 2a US zone is equivalent to a 0a in Canada. A 4b US zone is the same as a 6a zone in Canada. Here are some of the larger cities in Canada and their hardiness zones.

- Calgary, AB: 4a
- Edmonton, AB: 4a
- Halifax, NS: 6b

- Iqaluit, NU: 0a
- St. John's, NL: 5a
- Kelowna, BC: 7a
- Ottawa, ON: 5b
- Saskatoon, SK: 3b
- Toronto, ON: 7a
- Vancouver, BC: 8b
- Whitehorse, YT: 0b
- Yellowknife, NT: 0b

It is worth checking precisely what zone you are in as part of your planning. Like with the microclimates, just because the next town over is a 3a, it doesn't mean that your zone is going to necessarily be a 2b, 3a, or 3b.

NATIVE PLANTS THAT GROW WELL IN CANADA

Many of the plants native to Canada take a long time to actually reap the rewards of a bountiful harvest. Native plants are awesome but don't feel that this list is all you can grow. Not everyone has the patience to wait for years, me being one of them! For this reason, I have added a few extras that are not necessarily native but have been eaten by the Indigenous peoples in Canada for thousands of years and so are well-established and grow faster.

❖ Blueberries

At least 90 percent of the cultivated blueberries in Canada are grown in British Columbia because of the amazing soil conditions. However, blueberries also grow well in the wild. They can cope with partial shade but the fruit production will decline, so try to aim for full sunlight. Aside from having well-drained, loose soil, blueberries need an acidic soil with a pH level of 4.2 to 5.0. If you can get the ideal conditions, your blueberry bush can grow for around twenty years. A mature blueberry bush can produce around 5.5 to 7.7 pounds (2.5 to 3.5 kilograms) of berries.

There are five species of blueberry in Canada and they grow in Canadian Zones 3 to 6. Although they are easy to grow, it would be better to buy a young blueberry bush rather than growing from a seed. This is because they are a little sensitive to soil conditions. Plant the bushes at a distance of 3 to 4 feet and prune them back in winter when the bush is dormant.

❖ Giant puffball mushrooms

It's normal to feel dubious about picking mushrooms from the wild, especially if you aren't confident identifying them. Giant puffball mushrooms grow across Canada and other continents and are a traditional food of the Indigenous peoples. Fun fact: A researcher at Cornell University calculated that one 10-inch puffball can have seven trillion spores. If each spore grew to 10 inches, the combined mass would be

800 times that of the earth (Wild Food UK, 2015). Giant puffballs are easy to spot in the months from August to October and they can grow from 4 to 27 inches.

If you can harvest a giant puffball mushroom, you can use it to grow your own. Take a 5-gallon bucket of water and add 67 fluid ounces (2 liters) of mineral water. Break the puffball mushroom up as this will release the spores. Do this over the bucket so that the spores fall into the bucket. Add the broken-up pieces of mushroom to the water and add a pinch of salt and a tablespoon of molasses. The salt stops bacteria from growing and the molasses is the food source. Leave the bucket at room temperature for a maximum of two days and then pour the liquid onto the area you want your giant puff-balls to grow. Every couple of days, you will need to mist the area.

It takes just three to four weeks for these mushrooms to grow. Take a sharp knife and cut the stem at ground level. This way, the mushrooms will regrow next year.

✿ Canada lettuce

This plant can look quite weedy and sometimes even appear like dandelions. They have yellow flowers that turn into achenes that distribute in the wind. It's a tall lettuce that can grow to over 70 inches. Canada lettuce is fairly easy to grow because it isn't fussy when it comes to soil types. It does prefer the sun though.

Canada lettuce seeds can be sown directly into the ground or started in pots indoors. Because this type of lettuce is so hardy, it actually grows better outdoors. You can sow the seeds in spring, autumn, or both for a greater harvest. Only lightly cover the seeds in soil. Germination should only take between ten and twenty days, so it is a great choice for those who don't want to wait too long. Harvest the leaves and stems to eat when the plants are still young; leave them too long and the flavor becomes a little bitter.

✿ Wild leek

Wild leeks grow in the east, midwest, and northwest of Canada but it makes sense to grow them in your homestead garden because, in some places, there are strict rules on harvesting wild leeks and it is even protected in some parts. As long as you aren't breaking the law in your area, you can dig up one wild leek as they transplant well. Be sure to knock the soil off the roots because the soil contains dormant seeds. Your local nursery may also have wild leek plants.

Wild leeks also grow well from seeds but it will be two years before they sprout. Plant seeds about half an inch into the ground and 10 inches apart. Like morel mushrooms, they like soil conditions that mimic a forest floor, especially near deciduous trees, but with more sunlight. Wild leeks appear in early spring and are ready to harvest around May. Take advantage of every part of this delicacy.

❀ Asparagus

Technically, asparagus is native to southern Africa but as it grows so well in the wild across most of Canada, we have included this as a great option for your garden. Perfect soil temperatures are between 61°F and 86°F but asparagus also likes a winter frost or at least a cool season. The easiest way to grow asparagus is to plant the root or crown and you will be able to harvest the plant earlier, normally after two to three years.

Take the crowns of your asparagus and plant them 1 inch into the ground, 7 to 15 inches apart. Add compost or manure to the soil beforehand. The trick with asparagus is to take good care of them in the early years so that you get a rich yield for years to come. In spring, cut back any shoots larger than half an inch in diameter. During the summer, the asparagus will grow huge ferns, as tall as 5 to 6 feet, and bright red berries. Leave this to die down in the fall because it will provide nutrients for growth the following spring.

❀ Hazelnuts

Hazelnuts can be grown as a tree or a bush, depending on the amount of space you have. The American hazelnut and the beaked hazelnut are native to Canada, typically in Zones 2 to 5. The American hazelnut grows well from Manitoba to southwest Quebec whereas the beaked hazelnut will grow from British Columbia to Newfoundland. Bushes can grow up to 8 to 12 feet, trees up to 16 feet. They will produce nuts from year four and by year six or seven, you should be getting a heavy yield. The hazelnuts grow in pairs or small clusters.

Growing from a hazelnut is possible. Take a hazelnut with the shell and just nick the sides. Start by putting a layer of small stones in the bottom of a container for good drainage. Plant it in a container and cover it with a couple of inches of soil. By spring, the seed should have germinated and it's time to move it to a bigger container. When the young tree is two years old, you can plant it in its final spot. With hazelnuts, it's best to plant a wire mesh around the tree for protection from squirrels and deer.

✿ Wild rice

Wild rice or Canadian rice is the only cereal native to Canada and grows in wet, marshy areas so you will need a pond or other forms of water to grow it. It will need at least 4 inches of water all year round but the perfect depth is between 18 and 22 inches. It is best grown in Canadian Zones 6 and below although, if you are in warmer climates you can still grow it but it won't produce such an abundant yield.

Fall is the best time to plant wild rice. That being said, it's not really planting it. It's a case of throwing the seeds into the water. Seeds that are viable will sink to the bottom of the water and germinate. The seeds that aren't viable will float and become a food source for fish or wildlife. Germination occurs in spring, and four weeks later you will see leaves growing on the water's surface. Wild rice can reach a height of 12 feet. As you harvest the rice, seeds will fall into the water and the process starts again.

❀ High-bush cranberries

High-bush cranberries are a little sour and they smell a little off too. Nevertheless, they make excellent jams, sauces, and even wines, plus they are an attractive addition to any garden with the bush growing up to 15 feet. If you are planting multiple high-bush cranberries, keep 6 feet between each.

You can grow high-bush cranberries from the seed. Like other berries, you will need to clean the seeds and keep them in a cool place for around five months for them to germinate. Sow the seeds in spring in moist soil with full sun or partial shade. In June, you will see lovely white flowers and the fruit can be harvested from August to February but again, you will need a little patience as it will take approximately four years to bear fruit.

❀ Black walnuts

This tree is most successfully grown in southwestern Ontario where the ground is moist but they can be grown in hardiness Zones 4a to 6b and even Zone 7. This tree might be for the most patient of homestead gardeners as it can take eight to ten years to bear fruit and up to thirteen years if planted from the seed. However, it can live for up to 150 years.

To plant black walnut from the seed, remove all the husks and put the seeds in water. Those that sink should be kept and opened to check that the meat inside the nut is white and solid. The more seeds that are viable, the fewer seeds to plant per hole. If 80 to 100 percent were viable, you should have success with just two seeds per hole. If it's 40 to 60 percent, you are better off planting four seeds. You can plant the seeds in the fall or stratify them for 90 to 120 days.

❁ Fiddleheads

Aside from a cool name, fiddleheads are extremely healthy and the spiral shapes are unique for a vegetable. Fiddleheads belong to the fern family but it's the ostrich fern that is the most popular edible and the only native plant in Canada to have gained commercial success as a vegetable (The Canadian Encyclopedia, 2015). They can be grown all across Canada.

Fiddleheads need shade and well-drained soil. If you are struggling to find fiddleheads locally, you can harvest from the wild and transplant them. Make sure you harvest them between fall and spring while the plant is dormant. Plant the fiddlehead deep enough so that the dormant crown is just covered by soil. And compost once a year for the first two years. In year three, you can harvest the first crowns you planted and after, all can be harvested.

✿ Strawberries

There are three strawberry species that are native to Canada and grow in clearings, coastlines, meadows, and woodlands. The ideal zone for strawberries in Canada is 3b with soil temperatures of around 50°F to 68°F. The soil needs to be well-drained and you should start by adding some compost.

Strawberries are low-growing plants normally only reaching around 6 inches in height. Still, they have an almighty spread of 20 to 40 inches, so plant seeds at least 12 inches apart, preferably up to 40 inches apart. First, you will spot the 5-petaled flowers and then you should be looking at approximately eleven weeks of harvest. Watch out for the runners. These thin stems will take root and form new plants. You can cut the runner and leave the plant to grow or transplant the runner. It's always a good idea to keep a few runners in case your strawberry plant gets a virus and stops producing fruit.

The beauty of native plants is that if you see them growing in the wild, you know your chances of growing them in your garden are high. Before you start harvesting wild plants, always check what the local laws state. I have a few contacts later on that are great for native plants in Canada in case you aren't keen or can't harvest from the wild.

POLLINATORS THAT ARE NATIVE TO CANADA

You should keep your eyes open for 2 types of humming-birds in Canada. The rufous hummingbird is native to British Columbia, southern Yukon, and western Alberta. Males are often bright orange while females are green. They like to feast on flies, spiders, and wild columbines. The ruby-throated hummingbird is native from Alberta to Nova Scotia. They are actually green but get their names for the red patch on the male's throat. They transport pollen on their upper bodies.

The silvery blue butterfly is native to all parts of Canada but they especially like flowers that grow low to the ground in moist areas. You may also see Canadian tiger swallowtails and monarch butterflies in parts of Canada. They make excellent pollinators because they transport pollen on their legs and even their bodies. In terms of moths, you can find the hummingbird clearwing moth across most of Canada, except in Nunavut. Pollen tends to stick to their bodies as they visit open and deep flowers.

Native species of paper wasps are found in various parts of Canada but there is a greater variety of bees. I'm pleased that my super pollinator, the mason bee, is one of them. You may also see green sweat bees, bumblebees, polyester bees, and mining bees. Other helpful pollinators include the hoverfly and the checkered beetle.

Bear in mind there are still over 800 native pollinators in Canada (Government of Canada, 2021) so you certainly aren't limited to these. All of the native pollinators are essential for native plants, but if you are looking to plant something special for your pollinators, the next section has some choice ideas.

WHAT CAN YOU PLANT TO ATTRACT THE POLLINATORS?

With regard to choosing and planting your pollinator attractors, you probably know what I am thinking by now—check the packet because there may be different varieties and growing conditions.

- **Apples:** Apples are so versatile as food but they are necessary for pollinators too. The white and pale pink flowers smell sweet and attract bees, flies, and some species of butterflies. These insects require apple nectar and/or pollen for food.
- **Bee balm:** Although it's only native to parts of Canada, this amazing plant has large deep-pink flowers from mid to late summer. If you can grow bee balm, expect to see more bees, butterflies, flies, hummingbirds, moths, and wasps.
- **Columbines:** It's the shape of these flowers that amazes me. Blue columbine is a hardy native generally found in the north and west of Canada.

Blue columbines attract bees but it's the red columbine, native to eastern Canada, that hummingbirds are drawn to.

- **Canada lily:** Also known as the wild yellow lily, this plant likes moist soil and produces orange and yellow bulb flowers in summer. Collected from the wild, it can be toxic. In your garden, Canada lily can bring in butterflies, bees, and hummingbirds.

- **Lindley's aster:** Lindley's aster is great because it grows in a range of conditions from fields to thickets, woodlands, and even the roadside. Flowers can be purple or brown and blossom throughout summer. Bees and butterflies need Lindley's aster but so do pollinating insects like flies, wasps, moths, and beetles.

- **Red maple:** There are ten maples native to Canada and of course, the red maple is one. Red maple is important for pollinators because it is one of the first trees to produce flowers, so those early spring pollinators, particularly bees, head straight for this tree.

- **Prickly rose:** You will love the look of the prickly rose (Alberta Wild Rose) and you can use the rosehips to make teas and jellies. The low-maintenance perennial has open, pink flowers in May and June with a steady flow of bees, flies, and beetles.

- **Swamp milkweed:** As we have discussed the

importance of milkweed for the survival of monarch butterflies, I won't go into too much detail again. Expect shades of pink flowers from June to August.

FINDING A TRUSTED SOURCE FOR NATIVE CANADIAN SEEDS

If the laws allow it and you have easy access to native plants, you can take cuttings or transplant plants. Always be respectful of the environment and only take the minimum you need. If there is any risk of getting into trouble, my favorite resource is The Canadian Wildlife Federation because they have a list of native plant supplier profiles across the country.

Northern Wildflowers has seeds for the garden and seeds for restoring larger areas. You might be interested in the easy-to-grow wildflower seed mix but the site also has things like worm manure. All seeds are non-GMO and chemical-free. Finally, Nature's Garden Seed Company has native trees, wildflowers, organic vegetables, and a good range of seeds and seeded kits.

Now, if you really are desperate to start eating freshly grown fruits, nuts, and berries but aren't keen on waiting for years, you can take a look at Hardy Fruit Tree Nursery. The site has a lovely selection of established trees that have all been naturally grown. The nursery even has trees for Canadian hardiness Zone 1!

Another option to start growing native plants is to speak to your neighbors. It's actually quite funny how non-gardeners can have all sorts of plants growing in their gardens and they don't know what it is they are growing. There will also be other people who have planted natives and I can only imagine would be more than willing to give you some cuttings and even advice on growing. A seed or cutting swapping system is one of the best (and cheapest) ways to improve diversity in everyone's gardens.

8

TAKING ADVANTAGE OF THE INFAMOUS UK WEATHER FOR A SUSTAINABLE GARDEN

The UK, consisting of England, Scotland, Wales, and Northern Ireland, is approximately forty times smaller than the US. Surrounded by the North Sea, the North Atlantic Ocean, the Celtic Sea, and the English Channel, this island gets some interesting and rather harsh weather conditions.

On a positive note, the luscious green grass is nothing the movies can really capture. The wildlife is one of the first to benefit from the English weather. Before we look at what's native in the UK, it's important to understand the hardiness zones.

CAN THE US ZONES APPLY TO THE UK?

Really, this goes back to how the US hardiness zones are calculated. If you only consider the minimum temperatures, you can use the US numbers for the UK. In this case, the UK has zones from 7a to 10a with the majority of the UK in Zones 8a and 8b. This can still help us because we know that certain plants won't survive in these minimum temperatures.

Nevertheless, to give you a better idea of why average minimum temperatures are not enough to go on, parts of the south of the UK, Madrid, and Texas all fall under Zone 9, but the climate in each is very different.

We love the UK but, like the metric system and driving on the opposite side of the road, they like to have their unique system for understanding hardiness zones. In all fairness, the Royal Horticultural Society (RHS) has done a great job with the ratings that take into consideration not only average minimum temperatures but also daytime temperatures, coastal extremities, altitude, and shelter.

The UK hardiness system begins with H1a, H1b, and H1c. H1a needs temperatures warmer than 59°F (15°C). Plants are often of the tropical kind and need to be grown indoors or in a heated greenhouse. H1b plants similarly need to be grown in a heated greenhouse, indoors, or possibly outdoors in summer or warmer, sheltered areas. The temperatures are between 50°F and 59°F (10°C to 15°C). Temperatures between 41°F and 50°F (5°C to 10°C) can handle being grown outdoors in most of the UK as long as the daytime temperatures are warm enough.

After the H1 categories, we have H2 to H7. H2 plants can cope with low temperatures (34°F to 41°F / 1°C to 5°C) as long as there is no frost. H7 is for the hardiest of plants that can survive temperatures below −4°F (−20°C). Most of the UK falls into the H3 and H4 hardiness zones, similar to 7 and 8 in the US. My best advice is that if you are in the UK, try not to compare the US zones and focus instead on the UK hardiness zones because the staff at the RHS do know their stuff.

GROWING NATIVE EDIBLES IN YOUR UK GARDEN

The UK isn't necessarily famous for its long list of native fruits and vegetables. For this reason, some of the edibles in this list aren't technically classed as native to the UK but they do grow very well in the wild and so will make a nice addition to your UK garden.

❀ Wild raspberries

These delicious berries can be found in woodlands, hedgerows, and highlands all across the UK. The fruit can be harvested in summer and early autumn. Before the arrival of the fruit, wild raspberries have lovely five-petaled flowers but take advantage of this because they only keep their petals for a day.

The interesting thing about wild raspberries is that you get the same yield planting from the seed or a cutting but the quality of the fruit is better when you plant from a seed. Choose a spot in your garden that is well-drained, preferably in full sun and if not, partial shade. It's best to plant wild raspberry seeds in mid-winter because they need to chill before germination. Growth begins in mid-spring but it won't be until the following season that you will be able to harvest the fruit.

✿ Turnips

Turnips were originally found all across Europe and Asia but, as they grow so well in the wild across most of the UK hardiness zones, they made it onto the list. Plus, this is a fast-growing vegetable you will be able to see and taste your efforts a little quicker than other crops. Because it is a root crop, you need to check the soil for stones so that the growth isn't distorted.

A good location will be where manure has been added to the soil but not in the year prior to sowing turnip seeds. Turnips like full sun. You can start sowing seeds in March and stagger the sowing until August. This way you will have a longer harvest season. Plant seeds around 12 inches deep and 6 inches apart. The turnips will be ready to harvest six to ten weeks later. Waiting longer doesn't mean bigger turnips, just less flavor.

❀ Wild mustard

Different types of mustards are native to different parts of the world but England has a special relationship with this crop. Colman's, the English version of Heinz but mostly for mustards, has been using mustard seeds from two areas in England for over 200 years. It might be cheaper and easier to buy a jar of Colman's mustard—but where is the fun in that? Plus, mustard makes a great cover crop.

Mustard is easy to grow in practically any soil condition. They like the full sun even though they are a cool climate crop. In April, you can spread seeds onto the soil and just cover them with a sprinkling of soil and water, or you can plant seeds about half an inch into the ground and water. Seedlings will appear in as little as a week to ten days and yellow or white flowers, followed by the pods, in six weeks. As soon as the pods begin to turn light brown, they are ready to harvest.

❀ Wild gooseberries

England has a long history with gooseberries going back as far as the 13th century. They can be found in the wild in woodlands, hedgerows, and along the banks of rivers and streams. You can use gooseberries in jams and jellies, for wine, and to make facemasks. The flowers are very important for bees too.

You can grow gooseberries from the seed once you have soaked them in hot water and then dried them. If you have wild gooseberry bushes and you are allowed to take a cutting, you can also plant the cutting. Both will grow in the ground or, for smaller spaces, keep it in a container. After planting, there is little you need to do. Because gooseberries love the damp UK climate, you only have to water them in dry spells. Plant gooseberries from October to March. You may see fruit in the first year, however, it could take up to three years. You can harvest the fruit from June through to August. Gooseberries will need pruning when they are dormant.

❀ Wild cherries

Wild cherry is often seen as one of the most important native trees in the UK. Cherry is famous for its amazing spring blossom, which is an early source of nectar and pollen for insects and the cherries provide food for birds. It's not until the fourth year that a wild cherry tree produces fruit but it can live to be 50 to 150 years old.

To plant wild cherry from the seed (also called the pit or the stone), you need to soak the seeds and leave them to dry. Then store them in the fridge in an airtight container for fifty to seventy days. Plant the seeds in a container and leave them in a sunny place indoors until the last frost has passed. Once the seedlings reach 8 to 12 inches, they will be ready for transplanting to their permanent homes. Wild cherry trees should be pruned in winter or early spring before the fruit buds appear.

✿ Yarrow

Yarrow is actually a weed but I feel a little harsh labeling it this as it makes a delicious addition to salads, stews, soups, and even your fruit salads. Yarrow is one of those amazing plants for medicinal purposes too. A friend of mine put it straight onto a cut her husband had and it helped stop the bleeding as well as aiding in the healing of the wound. It is native to meadows, hedgerows, banks, and roadsides. You can find it in most parts of the UK, except for really wet areas. You need to be careful with yarrow as one plant can produce up to 6,000 seeds.

You can start growing yarrow seeds indoors six to eight weeks before the last frost. They will need to be in a place with plenty of light or the seeds won't germinate. In fact, this is the most difficult stage of growing yarrow. Germination should happen within fourteen to twenty-one days. Without the light, the seeds won't germinate and this is why some people prefer to buy a young plant. After that, the yarrow is not fussy with regard to the soil but does like full sunlight. Be sure to keep your yarrow cut back if you don't want it to become invasive.

✿ Sweet chestnuts

This could be one of these gifts that you give to your children but they may not appreciate it until they are adults themselves. Sweet chestnuts take around twenty-five years to bear fruit and then live up to 700 years. Some varieties take less time and of course, if you are planting a sweet chestnut tree, it won't take that long.

If you have sweet chestnut trees in your area, you can take one of the seeds that have fallen from the tree and plant it directly in the ground. To increase the chances of germination, you can store the seed in a cool place until the spiky husk breaks. Then, put the chestnut into compost or preferably peat moss and store it in the fridge for three months. In March, the seed can be planted indoors in 1 inch of soil and left in a warm sunny place. After around three months, you can transplant the seedling but be sure to gradually introduce it to the outdoors. It's worth putting a fence around the seedlings because some animals may try to dig up the nut.

✿ Oregon grapes

Technically, the Oregon grape is native to North America but it grows naturally in the UK and especially in Zone H5. The evergreen shrub has large green leaves that turn almost purple in winter. In spring, there are bright yellow flowers and the fruit can be picked throughout summer and fall. Despite the name, the fruit is a berry and not a grape. It's quite tart so best for jellies, jams, and curds.

The good news is that Oregon grape seeds can tolerate a wide range of soil types from chalk, loam, and clay to sand with a neutral pH. The plant also likes moist but well-drained soil. Oregon grapes like full or partial shade. As a shrub, the plant can get to 3 to 5 feet wide, so leave sufficient space if you are planting more than one. You will need to prune the plant in spring or once it has flowered.

THE MOST COMMON POLLINATORS IN THE UK

The most common pollinators in the UK are those that we have mentioned in the US and Canada but of course, the numbers will be different. When we talk about the number of species, we tend to cover Britain rather than the UK. This is because insects and birds don't exactly respect the border between the Republic of Ireland and Northern Ireland.

The RHS states there are over 260 species of solitary bees in Britain but there are also social bees like the honeybee and 24 bumblebee species. The numbers are similar for wasps with 7 species of social wasps, 250 species of solitary wasps, and a massive 6,000 species of parasitoid wasps.

There are approximately 6,500 fly species in Britain. The most common you are likely to see is one of the 270 species of the hoverfly, each one essential for pollination. Butterflies and moths are part of the Lepidoptera order. While there are more than 2,500 species of Lepidoptera native to Britain, fewer than 60 are butterflies. It's more likely that you will see moths like the brimstone, mother of pearl, or yellow-tail moths.

Ladybugs, soldier beetles, rose chafers, thick-legged flower beetles, and longhorn beetles are found across most of

Britain. However, flowers are visited by around 4,500 species of beetles.

NATIVE FLOWERS FOR YOUR POLLINATORS AND POSSIBLY YOUR RECIPES

I remember an English friend telling me about the first time her boyfriend bought her flowers. She was so impressed until he started eating them! The fact is, many flowers are not only edible but can also increase your nutrient intake. And of course, if you are entertaining a crowd, you can really show off your presentation skills. More importantly, you can provide native pollinators with all-important food and pollen.

- **Common columbine:** While Canada has its own columbine, so does the UK. It's not necessarily an abundant flower but it is widespread. The flowers are blue or purple and are often found with a white center. The flowers are edible but save a few for the butterflies.
- **Daisy:** There is no shortage of daisies in the UK but that's not to say you don't need them in your garden. Daisies are used for medicinal purposes and are often made into teas. The shape of a daisy makes them attractive to many pollinators but especially bees and butterflies.
- **Borage:** Borage is an annual but might survive a

second season in mild winters. Either way, it is self-seeding, so you won't need to replant it. The leaves and flowers are edible (I have seen fantastic cookies with the flower baked in). Borage attracts bumblebees, other native bees, and small wasps.

- **Trailing bellflower:** It's more common to find this flower in southern England but it does grow all over the UK. The violet flowers start off as bells but open up into star shapes. It attracts bees and butterflies but also other pollinating insects.

- **Foxglove:** Foxglove has been known to raise the dead and kill the living and while it has curative properties it is a poisonous plant, so don't stick it on your salad! Foxgloves can grow up to 12 feet and with pink/purple tube-shaped flowers. The sturdy tubes are a great landing pad for bumblebees.

- **Cowslip:** Just one stem of cowslip can have ten to thirty clusters of yellow flowers between April and May. They grow well across all parts of the UK. Cowslips are loved by bees and many other flying insects as well as beetles. The Duke of Burgundy butterfly is an endangered butterfly that relies on cowslip as a larval host plant.

- **Clover:** The UK is covered with clovers but it's the rare four-leafed clover that is said to bring luck. The white flowers of the clover are edible and can be found from May to October. Bees are attracted to white clover flowers, especially honeybees and bumblebees. They also provide food for the common blue butterfly.

- **Dandelion:** Like clover and cowslip, dandelions are found all over the UK. They are sometimes called tiddle-beds because of the myth that you wet the bed if you pick one. If the winter isn't too harsh, dandelions can bloom all year round. Various bee species like dandelions as well as beetles and birds.

It is likely that some of these plants are already growing in your garden. Because they are often seen as weeds people tend to pull them all up. It's true they don't make for an attractive lawn but you are doing an awesome job for the environment by letting them grow.

WHERE TO SOURCE YOUR SEEDS IN THE UK

The first place to start is the RHS. The site has seeds for sale but you can also take advantage of the free RHS gardening coach and an incredible amount of important information about our pollinators and the environment. For an extensive choice of plants, there is Landlife Wildflowers, which has seeds, bulbs, and plants. They have some fantastic seed mixes like the traditional meadow wildflower seed with twenty-three native species of wildflowers and grasses. They also have a section for bees and butterflies. British Wildflower Seeds has seed packets created for different counties and specific to hardiness zones. If you are looking for fruit and vegetable seeds Dobies has plenty to choose from including indoor and outdoor plants and sowing guides.

What is also great about the UK is the popularity of allotments and community gardens. Even if you don't have a garden, you can reach out and see if there are any spaces available or if there are some shared spaces you can contribute to.

Brexit has caused a bit of a shake-up for this little island and concerns for food supplies and prices don't seem to be easing. There is no better time than now to start growing your own food in the UK, and remember how grateful those pollinators will be.

9

MAINTAINING YOUR GARDEN WITHOUT PESTICIDES OR HERBICIDES

We are at the stage now where your garden design is complete. You have sectioned your area into zones and chosen the best elements for each zone. You should have observed the wildlife that visits your garden, the hours of sunlight, rain, etc. While you have plenty of ideas for companion plants, you are being very controlled and starting small!

Gardening is a little bit like the laundry, by the time you finish one load, there is another load to do. The difference is, your garden is far more rewarding. Nevertheless, even with the best designs, there will still be some maintenance. The soil has to have a continuous supply of food, weeds need to be managed, and we need to always be preparing for the following year. A splash of fertilizer and a quick spray is the easy solution but after all the effort to attract pollinators, it's not really fair to contaminate their new home.

It's natural to want to protect your fruits, vegetables, and flowers but there are other solutions to chemicals. These solutions help to create a natural balance where all elements can thrive and diversity is the focus.

WHAT'S WRONG WITH PESTICIDES AND HERBICIDES?

A pesticide is a broad term for chemical substances used to control plants or animals that are considered pests. There are four main types of pesticides:

- Herbicides: Used to kill weeds and other vegetation
- Insecticides: To control the impact of insects
- Fungicides: Substances that stop mold and mildew from spreading
- Disinfectants: For the control of bacteria

70 percent of conventionally grown fruits and vegetables contain up to 230 pesticides or pesticide breakdowns (Environmental Working Group, 2021). The EWG has a list called the Dirty Dozen that contains the twelve products that have the highest amounts of pesticides. At the top of the list is strawberries but the other eleven are also fruits and vegetables that we eat on a regular basis.

Pesticides can have horrendous consequences on our health and the environment. I don't want to go into these dangers because this isn't a lecture. Though I disagree with the use of such chemicals, I also understand that farmers struggle to make a living without them. That being said, farmers are working on a much larger scale than we are in our gardens, so our need to use sprays should be nonexistent.

THE IMPORTANCE OF MULCHING

Mulch is every homestead gardener's best friend. You can make organic mulch from a variety of materials and cover the soil. It is useful for different reasons but mainly the matter breaks down and adds nutrients to the soil. Mulch also helps to suppress weeds and keep moisture in the soil. Different materials have different properties. The drier the mulch, the longer it will take to decompose. You can buy mulch or use materials that you have in your home or garden. If you buy it, make sure it's chemical-free.

Mulch can be made out of bark or wood chippings. Grass clippings are a popular option for people who have a lawn. You can use the grass clippings wet or dry. If they are wet, only use a thin layer as they could mat down and prevent moisture from passing through. Wet grass clippings decompose faster than dry. Leaf mulch doesn't look all that attractive but it's highly effective. Instead of throwing out old newspapers, you can shred them or add a few sheets under another type of mulch. Spray the newspaper with water so that it stays in place.

For my vegetables, I love straw. Straw takes a long time to decompose so you probably only need to put down one layer prior to winter. I know it's all in the mind but I feel like it's a little blanket during the cold months. It will help protect the plants from diseases and provide those beneficial insects with some shelter.

You also have the option of living mulch, also known as cover crops. Living mulch can help to replenish nutrients and prevent soil erosion. Borage, nasturtium, comfrey, thyme, white clover, and mustard are excellent examples of living mulch but you can choose plants that will work well as companion plants for your garden. Living mulch also provides a nice home for insects.

PREVENTING PLANT DISEASE

There is a triangle of factors that can cause plant diseases. First, the host has to be susceptible to a disease, the pathogen must be capable of causing the disease, and finally, the environment has to be just right for that disease. If you can break the triangle, you can prevent diseases, although it is practically impossible to completely eliminate all diseases.

The soil is always a good place to start. It will help to test the pH of your soil so that you can choose the right plants—ones that will help to create a neutral balance. Compost and mulch will help with soil health. Try to include crop rotation in your long-term plan so that the soil has a chance to replenish.

Native plants tend to be more resistant to diseases. This is because the conditions are just right for them to thrive. You can also look at incorporating some disease-resistant plants into your plan. Again, I have to mention diversity. Remember how one rotten apple spoils the basket! If you have one rotten apple in a basket of oranges, the disease is contained to the apple. A loose example of course but certain plants are more susceptible to particular diseases. A wide range of plants can prevent diseases from spreading and destroying an entire garden.

Observation is also crucial for the health of your plants. As soon as you see any signs of disease you need to remove the diseased part. This means checking the leaves, flowers, and stems. Cut away any part showing signs of disease but don't put this on your compost heap. You risk spreading the disease across your garden. The earlier you find it, the better because diseases can be spread by the wind. The correct pruning of plants allows for healthy plant growth as well as the right amount of air circulation and light to get to all parts of the plant.

Water your plants in the morning. Plants are actually better at retaining water throughout the day. This also stops the plants from sitting in water overnight, which can increase the chances of disease. Water the soil around plants and not the leaves. The leaves are the most susceptible to diseases, plus if there are droplets when the sun comes out, the leaves could burn.

INTEGRATED PEST MANAGEMENT

Integrated pest management (IPM) is a strategy that looks at controlling pests in different ways but naturally is always the first choice. As an absolute last resort, chemicals would be used, however, IPM begins with biological controls and changing habitats to make conditions unappealing for pests. Let's start with biological control and natural enemies!

Going back to our companion plants, there are some excellent options to help with pest control. As you have probably guessed, the list is quite extensive but here are some ideas for common pests you might encounter.

- Oregano with broccoli: Keeps cabbage moths away
- Borage with tomatoes: Borage deters tomato hornworm and attracts bees
- Parsley with asparagus, carrots, tomatoes, and roses: Repels carrot flies and beetles
- Pennyroyal: Part of the mint family, it deters gnats, mosquitos, ants, and cabbage maggots
- Rosemary and sage: Carrot flies and cabbage moths don't like rosemary or sage

Another good idea is to plant radish, even if you don't like it yourself. Radish sprouts quickly and insects munch on the radish and leave the other seedlings in peace for healthy growth.

We need to control pests but, at the same time, we want to encourage a wide range of insects to help with pollination. Another strategy in IPM is to introduce animals and insects that control other pests. A classic example is to introduce a chicken or duck if you have a problem with slugs. Some of our favorite pollinators also act as natural pest controllers.

Ladybugs are adorable to look at, but not if you are a pest. They are famous for eating aphids. Like human teenagers, ladybug teenagers have quite an appetite. They can eat hundreds of aphids in a day. They will also take care of mites and other small pests. Hoverflies and parasitic wasps also eat aphids and soft-bodied pests while ground beetles eat practically any pest.

To encourage these highly beneficial insects, plant different flowers (especially nasturtiums for ladybugs), have a small stack of bricks or pile of wood for them to take shelter, and don't forget a dish of water with stones so that they can safely drink.

SANITIZING YOUR TOOLS

I confess, in my early homestead gardening days this never crossed my mind but it is so logical. We are all aware of the importance of disinfecting our home, kitchen surfaces, etc., but it makes sense that our gardening tools can come into contact with bacteria and diseases. If we don't sanitize them, chances are the disease spreads when we use the tools on other plants.

People have different methods of sanitizing tools. I have heard of people using vinegar. Vinegar will kill some microbes but have no effect on others, so there is no guarantee. Isopropyl alcohol is more effective but some people find the smell too strong and you have to be careful because it can be flammable.

I use good old-fashioned bleach. Make a bleach solution using one part bleach and nine parts water. In a bucket, add your tools to the solution and let them soak for up to thirty minutes. Clean off any mud or soil that is stuck to the tools first. Rinse the tools with water and dry them properly to prevent rust.

This should be done every time you work on a different plant but we know this isn't practical. Try to do it after every gardening session, especially if you have seen evidence of disease.

CONTROL THE WEEDS

I feel sorry for weeds. Like pests, they too have a right to grow but they also have a tendency to be a nuisance. First of all, identify your weeds and decide if they are providing some form of benefit to your garden or your pollinators. Do you really need to get rid of them? Of course, if the weeds are getting out of control, then action will have to be taken.

One of the most important areas to weed is around your fruits and vegetables. Weeds that pop up here are going to compete for the nutrients in the soil and you want your edibles to get the most out of the soil as they can.

Smothering weeds is a good option. We have already seen how mulch can help prevent weeds from popping up, as can newspapers. Even a layer of compost stops sunlight from reaching the seeds and germination from occurring. Just be very careful with mulch and compost if you are making your own. A rookie mistake I made was to throw my weeds onto the compost heap. The next thing I know, I am spreading weed seeds all across my garden!

Take advantage of every space when planting your fruits, vegetables, and flowers. As the plants grow, they will block out the light and this will stop weeds from growing around them. That being said, you can't plant things too close together or else they will also start competing for nutrients and light. This is yet another reason why companion plants are so helpful.

You can cut your weeds by at least half just by watering your garden selectively. Only water what you want to grow. It can also cut down on your water usage. This strategy may not work for deep-rooted weeds as they still have access to water deeper in the soil.

You may have heard of tilling. I used to be a fan because turning over the topsoil was like fluffing it up. Not only did it look nicer but it also helped to circulate air through the soil. To till or not to till is up to you but most of the soil in your garden will contain weed seeds. As soon as you till the soil, these seeds become exposed to the sunlight and can germinate. Tilling can also disrupt the microbes in the soil. My advice is to only till or dig the areas that you need to prepare for planting.

DON'T WASTE YOUR CROPS

It goes without saying that after the effort you have made to grow your food, you really don't want to waste it. If you don't harvest your crops at the right time, you risk wasting the food. You might be tempted to leave something to grow until it is a little bigger but in reality, it will either lose quality or start to rot. Some people struggle to harvest their food because they become like their babies. After taking care of these plants and watching them grow for so long it is hard to eat them. Don't worry—more will grow! When you harvest food, the plant knows that it is time to produce more food.

Succession sowing is perfect for reducing waste. Let's say you want a winter harvest of carrots, you can sow seeds in September and October. If you sow seeds every week or two, you will have a fresh harvest of carrots every couple of weeks. This is better than harvesting all your carrots at once and not knowing what to do with them all.

When your seedlings start to sprout, you may need to thin them out. Rather than throwing these separated seedlings onto the compost heap, share them with others. They don't need to be an avid gardener to appreciate a new plant. You may even pass the gardening bug onto someone else. If you have other gardening enthusiasts or you are working in an allotment, share these seedlings with others so that they can increase the diversity in their gardens. They will probably return the favor!

Any excess food that you aren't going to eat or preserve should be donated. See which friends and family can get the most out of your crops and, if there are still leftovers, take it down to your local soup kitchen. Don't forget that all of your kitchen scraps can go straight onto the compost heap and turn into food for the next season.

If you feel like there is too much work, it might be that you haven't quite mastered the right balance. Don't worry, few gardeners do this in their first or even second season. It just means that your plan needs a little bit of adjustment so that your elements are helping to take care of each other. Take a closer look at your companion plants and introduce both annuals and perennials. Rather than planting more, you may want to consider planting something different to see if you can reach your objectives.

10

PUTTING YOUR 'BEDS TO BED' READY FOR SPRING

Homestead gardening isn't over after the harvest. Your pantry and freezer may well be fully stocked but there is still plenty to do. Many plants will go dormant over winter and it feels like a moment for you to let sleeping plants be. Don't forget that you have created a perfect home for pollinators and your responsibility doesn't hit pause. Plus, what you do now is going to help improve all of the elements in your garden.

Now is the ideal time to start getting things ready for the next season. The first thing you can do is collect the seeds of the crops you want to plant in the next season. They can be kept in envelopes in a dry place. Be sure to dry the seeds out properly before you store them. If not, they may not germinate when you plant them. While you are collecting seeds, take a good look for any diseased or damaged parts of plants and cut these back now. Regardless of what type of plant or the time of year, diseased and damaged parts of a plant need to be removed.

Your perennials need to be cut back as soon as they start to lose their leaves. Cut them back to the stem and leave about 6 inches of the stem in place. Some people pull up the roots of annuals but it's more beneficial to leave them in the ground. Cut your annuals back to ground level and let the roots be eaten by worms, bacteria, and other organisms, converting the dead roots back into nutrients for the soil. There are others who will leave the entire plant in place because, like the roots, they will rot and provide nutrients. At the same time, they will help reduce soil erosion and give some much-needed shelter to your pollinators. To pull or not to pull is your choice but take advantage of the dying plants one way or another. Left in the soil, composted, or used as mulch, there are valuable nutrients that are far better than fertilizers.

While you are in inspection mode, take a closer look at those weeds. So many gardeners will tell you that before putting your garden bed to bed for winter, you should get rid of those weeds. Most definitely pull up those weeds that are around your edibles. Think carefully about the weeds that are good for pollinators and if they can do more good than harm. For bare soil, I find it is best to leave these weeds in place as a cover crop. It doesn't make sense to pull up weeds only to spend money on cover crops.

Next, you will really need your compost! Cover your garden beds with an inch or two of compost so that the soil is well-fed. Most people think that this task is best left for spring but adding these nutrients now allows time for the matter to break down and release those nutrients. Everything you have cut back can then be put on top of the compost as a layer of mulch. Fallen leaves make excellent mulch so there is no need to chuck them on the compost heap and definitely not in the trash. Add them straight onto the soil for mulch. Not only is this going to feed your soil but it will also help to protect your garden from frost.

It's the last time I will say this but check the seed packet for winter care! Some herbs will cope with winter outdoors, others may need to be brought inside or covered. Most perennials can be cut back, however, those like cone-flowers and rudbeckia can be left to cut back in spring because the birds can feed off the seeds in winter. Your hardy vegetables may even taste better with a touch of frost.

There isn't really one rule that fits all for preparing a garden for the next season. Taking the above steps will be the ideal way to let your soil rest and replenish so that when the spring sun starts to warm your garden up, you will have the best conditions to start the new season.

Of course, now is also the time to give yourself a pat on the back and marvel at what you have achieved. You are probably feeling very motivated about spring and have thought of some new plants that you want to include. Get excited and go back to the drawing board to plan for the next season.

And for some, they follow the instructions to a T, yet things still don't seem to go their green way! In the final chapter, we will find the answers to some of the most common home-stead gardening problems so that your garden is sustainable, bountiful for all, and a beauty to admire.

11

TROUBLESHOOTING—WHAT ON EARTH IS GOING WRONG?

Years ago, I was so delighted with the success of my little balcony that as soon as I moved into my first house with a garden I couldn't wait to become a "real" gardener. After doing everything right, seedlings didn't sprout, flowers didn't blossom, there were no vegetables and no pollinators. It's like whatever green magic I had on the balcony had stayed there and I was a novice all over again.

There is always going to be a learning curve. Each time you plant something new, there will be a chance to learn. Some of our knowledge can be transferred to other areas of the garden. Sometimes it feels like we do everything right but don't get the results. For this reason, I have put together this troubleshooting chapter. Here, we will address some of the common issues homestead gardeners have and some tips and tricks on how to overcome them.

How can I make my own compost?

Making your own compost is easy and so beneficial. You can reduce your household waste and feed your garden too. There are a few different ways to make your own compost but you will always need four things: carbon, nitrogen, water, and oxygen. Carbon comes from the brown materials you add, like dried leaves, and the nitrogen comes from your greens, such as lawn clippings and kitchen scraps.

You can section off an area in your garden and use this as the compost heap by adding a fence around it. If you have more space, you can use the three-bin system. When your first heap is full, it gets turned into the second bin and then finishes off in the third bin. Alternatively, a large plastic bin works just as well. I drilled a lot of holes in the base and sides of my bin and rested it on a few bricks. It's easy to take the lid off to water and I can roll it on the ground to turn the contents.

There are also machines that you can keep in your kitchen and easily just throw all of your kitchen scraps into. They are a little pricey but another excellent solution for those who need to see results a little quicker—in fact, a lot quicker. You can have compost in as little as two days.

What can't go on the compost heap?

Don't put meat or fish products on your compost heap, there is a risk of it smelling rather horrible and attracting pests. The same goes for dairy products and any cat or dog waste.

Fats and oils can slow down the composting process. Aside from this, be careful not to put any diseased plants, anything infected with pests, and seeding weeds. Ash from wood can help balance out the acidity but ash from charcoal might have chemical residues, and you don't want to put anything on the compost heap that has chemicals.

I don't feel excited about anything that grows in my hardiness zone. Is it really impossible to plant things out of my zone?

Remember the hardiness zones are just general guidelines but they are incredibly useful for starting out. We have also learned how it's not only the minimum winter temperature that needs to be considered. You also have the option of growing things indoors. This might require more work because you will need to bring your plants in at night. Once the sun comes out and the temperatures are equal to or above your indoor temperatures, you can place them outside to get the benefits of the natural light and fresh air. When those temperatures start to drop, bring them back in. There are also options like polytunnels and greenhouses if you have the space. You can also use heating lamps and mats to help with germination and stronger seedlings.

Nevertheless, and maybe this is just me, but I think it's important that gardeners get good at growing the things that nature provides us with before attempting the more exotic options. A helpful rule to stick to is that perennials can handle slightly lower zones and annuals a little higher than what is shown on the charts.

How can I check the soil quality in my garden?

If your plants aren't growing well it's a good sign that there is an issue with your soil quality. However, you don't want to use this as your test because you might have wasted an entire year. There are plenty of soil pH testing kits that you can buy online. While they are an inexpensive investment it's not the most fun because there are homemade tests that work!

Put 2 tablespoons of soil in a bowl and add half a cup of vinegar. If the soil starts to fizz it means your soil is on the alkaline side. If you add half a cup of baking soda to 2 table-spoons of moist soil (add some distilled water if need be) and the soil fizzes, it is acidic. If there is no reaction to either, you know that your soil is pH neutral.

My granny keeps telling me to pinch the fruit and I have no idea what she is talking about. Why and how should you pinch fruit?

Pinching is a form of pruning but like a mini version that doesn't require any cutting tool. It's an important practice because it helps them grow into a fuller, bushier plant. By pinching the stem just above the leaf nodes, you remove the new growth and two new stems grow. It is especially impor-tant to pinch herbs because you can get more leaves. Also, imagine you have a tomato plant: the more stems you have, the more tomatoes you can enjoy.

We pinch young plants. A seedling needs to have a few pairs of leaves on the stems before you pinch it. If you look closely at the base of a leaf, you will see the bud. You need to pinch the stem just above this bud so that the plant receives the message to begin new growth. It will only take a couple of days for you to see the new stems growing. Once these stems have a few pairs of leaves, you can pinch out this new layer of growth.

Why are my plant leaves turning yellow?

One of the most common reasons for leaves turning yellow is a watering issue. The same applies if you notice the leaves starting to droop. Not enough water is what we often assume but the same thing can happen with overwatering. If you place a finger on the soil and the soil sticks, this is a good sign that your soil has the right moisture. You can also stick your finger about 2 to 3 inches into the soil to test further below.

The plant may also not be getting enough light. In this case, you should move it and monitor the leaves. In any case, the yellow leaves are unlikely to return to green, so you should remove them to keep the plant healthy.

How do I know my plants are getting the right nutrients?

It's all in the leaves and close observation. The first thing I would recommend is checking that your plants are getting the right amount of water because this can help resolve curling, yellow, droopy, and somewhat sad-looking plants. After that, we need to think about possible signs of malnutrition that you can see from the leaves.

For example, another reason for leaves to turn yellow is that there is a lack of magnesium and iron in the soil or your soil could be too acidic. If plants are growing weak and they appear spindly, there is too much nitrogen in the soil. Brown or shriveled leaves could be a sign of a lack of potassium.

Many people would tell you to fertilize your plants better, but we are aiming for a more natural approach. Even then, fertilizer brings its own issues. Brown spots on your leaves and stems can be a sign of fertilizer burn. This is why I prefer a combination of my own compost and mulch so I know exactly what's going back into my plants.

My young plants are dying. What am I doing wrong?

Again, the first thing to do is check how much water and light they have. It's quite easy to stress young plants out by not giving them the right conditions. If you are covering seedlings, make sure the cover comes off on a regular basis so that there is enough air ventilation too.

A common problem for young plants is damping off. This is a disease that involves different types of fungi. The seedlings collapse just at soil level and you might notice white fungi around the base of the stem. Sadly, there is no cure for young plants affected by damping off. The plant and soil have to be discarded (and not on the compost heap). Start fresh and with good quality potting soil and be extra careful of the light, air, and water your plants are getting. It's high humidity that will encourage damping off. Use water from your faucets instead of rainwater. If you are going to reuse the containers, you will need to disinfect them before planting new seeds.

When people talk about pruning I imagine Edward Scissorhands. How do I prune correctly?

It is easy to get carried away with pruning. I have had moments when I chopped a bit off from here and then the plant looked too overgrown on one side and before I knew it, the plant had had a serious "haircut." If there are any dead parts or diseased and damaged areas, the plant should be pruned straight away, regardless of the time of year. Plants generally prefer to be pruned in late winter or early spring. It's best to check exactly when your plants should be pruned but here is a quick guide:

- Flowering trees, shrubs, and vines: Late winter or early spring
- Fruit trees and berries: When they are dormant
- Evergreens: Never, or a very small amount in early spring
- Perennials: Spring or fall

Again, a very general rule is to cut one-third off the end of the stems. But if you have a fruit tree that has grown more than 2 feet, you need to cut this back because it's unlikely that you will get fruit in the following season. If there are branches that have grown across another branch, it's wise to cut them back too because they will prevent good air circulation.

Take a sharp tool, scissors, or secateurs. Find the node on the branch or stem. This is the knobbly bit where the leaves and buds grow from the stem. Cut just above the node at a 45-degree angle facing downward. This will let rainwater run off rather than sit on the wound and increase the risk of infections. Only remove 10 to 20 percent of the plant. If you need to prune more, wait at least ten days. Unless the plant can handle a hard prune (cutting the entire plant back to between 6 and 12 inches) you are likely to cause more bad than good.

Only half of my seeds have sprouted. What could be the problem?

It's a bit of a heartbreaking situation. You are so excited to see your seedlings sprout but it might be a case of only a few containers sprouting, half of them, or none at all. Don't give up, a few things just need to be changed. The goal is for 80 to 90 percent of your seedlings to germinate. If this doesn't happen, there might be a problem.

The quality of your seeds is a good place to start. If they weren't dried out before being stored, the seeds might have rotted. During storage, they also need to be kept in a cool place. Anything over 90°F will kill the seed. This is why I recommend trusted nurseries to buy seeds because they will have harvested them and stored them correctly.

After that, it goes back to the conditions. Perhaps the soil was infected, which is why you should always start with fresh soil. If you are reusing soil, you can bake it on grease-proof paper for thirty minutes at 180°F. This will kill off anything that could harm your seeds.

Try to keep the soil temperature consistent. High or low temperatures won't help with germination but extreme changes may also affect how many of the seeds germinate. Finally, when it comes to water, try using a mister to keep the soil moist but not drown the seeds.

I'm not getting any fruit yield yet. What could be the problem?

Our fruit trees, along with nuts and berries require the most amount of patience. Many times, the plant won't be producing fruit because it hasn't matured yet. Growing from a seed is so rewarding but choosing a mature plant from a local nursery will speed up that wait.

In the case of fruit trees, you really do want to observe and follow the hardiness zones because if it is too cold, the fruit won't appear. Too much nitrogen is another cause for fruit not to appear. When you are adding mulch, try to keep the mulch around fruit trees to brown residues (dried leaves and straw) rather than green.

Finally, check that your plant type isn't self-sterile. Apples, pears, and sweet cherries are just some examples of plants that won't produce fruit if planted individually. You will need to plant in pairs for pollination to occur.

If you are getting fruit but it is small or there is not much fruit growing, you need to go back and check that the trees are getting enough water and add aged mulch or compost to keep the soil rich in nutrients.

What are some good plants to have in your homestead garden for medicinal purposes?

We looked at how yarrow can help with healing cuts and wounds but there are so many plants, mainly herbs, that the insects, our little pollinator friends, will love too.

- **Rosemary:** An anti-inflammatory and anti-bacterial
- Aloe vera: Skin problems such as rashes, sunburns, and stings
- **Valerian:** Relaxant, helps improve sleep and ease indigestion
- **Beth root:** Indigestion and some breathing problems like asthma
- **Allheal:** As an anti-inflammatory and anti-microbial, it lives up to its name
- **St. John's Wort:** Has been known to help with anxiety and depression as well as being anti-bacterial
- **Lemon balm:** Antioxidant, helps relieve stress, anxiety, heartburn, and indigestion
- **Oregano:** Can help to boost the immune system

Before you start using any plant for its medicinal purposes, check with your doctor first, especially if you are taking other types of medication. Despite being natural remedies, even some medicinal plants can cause reactions.

Close observation will really help you to master these common problems. As you are watering your plants, take the time to check the soil, leaves, and stems for any signs of early issues. Even if you don't have to water the garden, have a quick inspection to ensure everything is growing in the right direction. After all, your garden is there to be admired!

CONCLUSION

There is no better addiction to have than homestead gardening. I've seen gardens covered in tiles and not an inch of green, others covered in windchimes and interesting gnome collections. Each one has its individual beauty, but it's a homestead garden that I see and feel such a connection with. The planned wilderness makes you feel like you are so close to nature and, when you take a closer look, you see all the beneficial things that are going on.

Our basic needs are food, shelter, air, and water, all of which we can get from nature as long as we take care of our environment. In a perfect world, every human would respect the fact that nature provides us with sufficient resources and that greed leads to such an imbalance that causes devastating natural disasters. As we don't live in this perfect world, it's up to us to do what we can with the space we have.

Before reading this book, you may have come up with a list of things that you want to grow because these are the fruits and vegetables that you like to eat. Now, after understanding natives and hardiness zones, you might feel that your original list isn't appropriate. The truth is, palm trees grow in Scandinavia and even winter-hardy vegetables can grow in hot climates. The main point is that it will take a certain level of practice to do this.

For beginners, it just makes more sense to start with things that you know are going to grow well and easily in your area. There is a very good reason why schoolchildren grow alfalfa sprouts in eggshells rather than orchids—it's easy, the results are fast to see, and the children can feel confident. Apply the same theory to your garden!

With all the studies and statistics, I hope you find a special place in your garden or even on your balcony for the pollinators. They too need food, water, air, and shelter for their survival but, without them, we will see more and more struggles to provide enough food for the growing global population. Some pollinators might be pests and love to munch on your beautiful green leaves. Try to take this as a compliment and, rather than get out those nasty sprays, provide them with their own little buffet in your garden.

Diversity is every homestead gardener's best friend. Having a wide range of plants, flowers, fruits and vegetables, annuals, and perennials are going to attract more pollinators. It is also going to help you have a longer and more abundant harvest, possibly even year-round food for all. Your soil will thank you for this diversity and diseases won't spread and cause as much damage as when there are just a couple of crops.

That being said, starting out in your first year by planting twenty or thirty different plants may well backfire. The first year is a massive learning curve and it should be a fun one, not a stressful one. Attempting to grow too much without the correct observation could be a recipe for disaster and, in the worst-case scenario, put you off gardening for good. Learn from your first season and add more each year. Your patience will pay off, I promise.

Once you see those first seeds sprouting, you will appreciate that homestead gardening isn't difficult. However, it does require a lot of planning and organization. Even after my years of gardening now, I am still a huge fan of apps that help with all this planning and, before the existence of all these apps, I relied on a separate calendar just for the garden. For many of us, we still have a number of other responsibilities and it's easy to forget what gets sown, when it's time to replant, and when it's time to harvest.

Homestead gardening is a healthy hobby that brings bountiful rewards. It's something you can do with a friend, a partner, your parents, or get your children inspired. The more the merrier, and a bit of gardening competition is also healthy, especially if you follow the ethics of sharing your produce, seeds, and cuttings. Share your knowledge and your successes, because this is what is going to help others lead a more sustainable life.

I wanted to write this book because I have learned so much and not always the easy way! But there is more to it than that. I genuinely believe that anyone can grow their own food and create a home for pollinators when they have the right tools, specifically, the information. What's more, if you are giving pollinators a safe and welcoming home, they will help your garden grow and create an abundant harvest for years to come. Now it's your turn to start helping the environment by planning your homestead garden. Still, there is one more thing you can do that may not seem like a huge help to the environment but you will be surprised. There are other like-minded people nervous and overwhelmed about homestead gardening. By leaving a review for this book on Amazon, you can help reassure them that they can do it too! I will also be eternally grateful. Until then, happy gardening and good luck!

Just For You

As a way of saying thank you for your purchase, I am offering you an additional very useful list of fruits, vegetables, companion plants, pollinator-loving plants, and pollinators to kickstart your own year-round garden that will bring you abundant harvests every month of the year.

Scan this code to receive instant access to *Companion Planting Chart for Fruits, Vegetables, and Pollinators*. I look forward to sharing your homestead and pollinator gardening journey with you.

REFERENCES

Aubrey, A. (2013, February 20). *Smaller But Better? Organic Tomatoes May Pack More Nutritional Punch*. NPR. https://www.npr.org/sections/thesalt/2013/02/19/172416458/smaller-but-better-organic-tomatoes-may-pack-more-nutritional-punch?t=1637590126391&t=1641218392860

Biggane, E. (2019, November 11). *The Puffballs*. Wild Food UK. https://www.wildfooduk.com/articles/the-puffballs/

Bird Life International. (2021). *BirdLife Data Zone*. http://datazone.birdlife.org/2021-annual-update

Canadian Wildlife Federation. (n.d.). *Explore Our Pollinators*. https://cwf-fcf.org/en/resources/encyclopedias/fauna/explore-our-pollinators.html

Cekander, C. (2016, October 3). *Hazelnut Trees Are Easy!* Cornell Small Farms. https://smallfarms.cornell.edu/2016/10/hazelnut-trees-are-easy/

Coelho, S. (n.d.). *28 Powerful Medicinal Plants to Plant in Your Garden.* Morning Chores. https://morningchores.com/medicinal-plants/

da Silva, L. (2014, May 13). *Flower Visitation by Birds in Europe.* Wiley Online Library. https://onlinelibrary.wiley.com/doi/10.1111/oik.01347

Datta, S. (2021, August 29). *Pollinator Numbers Are Falling Around the World—But for Different Reasons.* The Wire Science. https://science.thewire.in/environment/pollinators-decline-too-few-studies-south-asia-africa-risk-for-humans/

Environmental Working Group. (2021, March 12). *EWG's 2021 Shopper's Guide to Pesticides in Produce.* EWG. https://www.ewg.org/foodnews/summary.php

European Parliament. (2021, June 9). *What's Behind the Decline in Bees and Other Pollinators?* https://www.europarl.europa.eu/news/en/headlines/society/20191129STO67758/what-s-behind-the-decline-in-bees-and-other-pollinators-infographic

Garce, K. (2021, June 5). *Organic Onions vs. Regular Onions: What's the Difference?* Food Storage, Choices and Alternatives. https://foodsforantiaging.com/organic-onions-vs-regular-onions-whats-the-difference/

Gardenate. (n.d.). *Growing Strawberry Plants.* https://www. gardenate.com/plant/Strawberry%20Plants?zone=59

Good, K. (2020, December 29). *Toxin Alert! Common Pesticides Used on Produce and How They Impact Humans and the Environment.* One Green Planet. https://www.onegreenplanet.org/ environment/pesticides-used-on-produce-and-how-they-impact-humans-and-the-environment/

Government of Canada. (2021, June 29). *Pollinator Protection.* https://www.canada.ca/en/health-canada/services/ consumer-product-safety/pesticides-pest-management/ growers-commercial-users/pollinator-protection.html

Hansen, J. (2018). *An American Timeline: Home Gardening in the US.* GardenTech.com. https://www.gardentech.com/ blog/gardening-and-healthy-living/an-american-timeline-home-gardening-in-the-us

Johnston, N. (2011, August 2). *15 Wild Plants You Can Eat.* Outdoor Canada. https://www.outdoorcanada.ca/15-wild-plants-you-can-eat/

Laganda, G. (n.d.). *2021 Is Going to Be a Bad Year for World Hunger.* United Nations. https://www.un.org/en/food-systems-summit/news/2021-going-be-bad-year-world-hunger

National Interagency Fire Center. (n.d.). *Statistics.* https:// www.nifc.gov/fire-information/statistics

Oliveira, A. B. (2013, February 20). *The Impact of Organic Farming on Quality of Tomatoes Is Associated to Increased Oxidative Stress during Fruit Development*. PLOS ONE. https://journals.plos.org/plosone/article?id=10.1371/journal.pone.0056354

Para Space. (n.d.). *Plant Hardiness Zones in Canada: How Do They Work?* https://www.paraspaceinc.com/blog/plant-hardiness-zones

Price, M. (2021, March 24). *What a USDA Hardiness Zone Is and Why It's Crucial for Keeping Your Plants Alive*. CNET. https://www.cnet.com/home/yard-and-outdoors/what-is-hardiness-zone-map-us-usda/

RHS. (n.d.-a). *Pollinators: Decline in Numbers*. Royal Horticultural Society. https://www.rhs.org.uk/wildlife/pollinators-decline-in-numbers

RHS. (n.d.-b). *RHS Hardiness Rating*. Royal Horticultural Society. https://www.rhs.org.uk/plants/trials-awards/award-of-garden-merit/rhs-hardiness-rating

Ros, M. (2017, January 25). *Spain's Ancient Olive trees: New Taste for Old Flavor*. CNN. https://edition.cnn.com/travel/article/millenary-olive-trees-spain/index.html

Shattuck, A. (2012, January 1). *We Already Grow Enough Food for 10 Billion People… and Still Can't End Hunger*. Food First. https://foodfirst.org/publication/we-already-grow-enough-food-for-10-billion-people-and-still-cant-end-hunger/

Small, E. (2015, March 23). *Fiddleheads*. The Canadian Encyclopedia.   https://www.thecanadianencyclopedia.ca/en/
article/fiddleheads

Smithsonian. (n.d.). *Butterflies in the United States*. Smithsonian   Institution.   https://www.si.edu/spotlight/
buginfo/butterflyus

Stevens, A. (2020, December 3). *Around the World, Birds Are in
Crisis*.   Science   News   for   Students.   https://www.
sciencenewsforstudents.org/article/bird-decline-global-
crisis

Stritongchuay, T. (2019, October 1). *The role of bats in pollination networks is influenced by landscape structure*. ScienceDirect.
https://www.sciencedirect.com/science/
article/pii/S2351989419302422

3 Simple DIY Soil Tests. (2021, November 12). Almanac.com.
https://www.almanac.com/content/3-simple-diy-soil-tests

United Nations. (2009). *The State of Food Insecurity in the
World; Economic Crises — Impacts and Lessons Learned. Food and
Agriculture* Organization of the United Nations

https://www.fao.org/3/i0876e/i0876e.pdf

United Nations. (2019, May 6). *UN Report: Nature's Dangerous
Decline   'Unprecedented';   Species   Extinction   Rates
'Accelerating.'* United Nations Sustainable Development.
https://www.un.org/sustainabledevelopment/blog/2019/
05/nature-decline-unprecedented-report/

University of California, Division of Agriculture and Natural Resources. (n.d.). *Meet The Pollinators*. University of California. https://ucanr.edu/sites/PollenNation/Meet_The_Pollinators/

US Forest Service. (2021). *Animal Pollination*. United States Department of Agriculture. https://www.fs.fed.us/wildflowers/pollinators/animals/

USGS. (2020, July 23). *How Many Species of Native Bees Are in the United States? | U.S. Geological Survey*. https://www.usgs.gov/faqs/how-many-species-native-bees-are-united-states?qt-news_science_products=0#qt-news_science_products

Woods, J. (2021, June 24). *US Beekeepers Continue to Report High Colony Loss Rates, No Clear Progression Toward Improvement*. Auburn University. https://ocm.auburn.edu/newsroom/news_articles/2021/06/241121-honey-bee-annual-loss-survey-results.php

World Health Organization. (2021, June 9). *Malnutrition*. https://www.who.int/news-room/fact-sheets/detail/malnutrition

Wright, M. (2012, June 29). *How Local Farmers Saved English Mustard*. Great Food Club. https://www.greatfoodclub.co.uk/how-local-farmers-saved-english-mustard/

Made in the USA
Columbia, SC
02 August 2022

64462733R10105